SENSITIVE SKIN

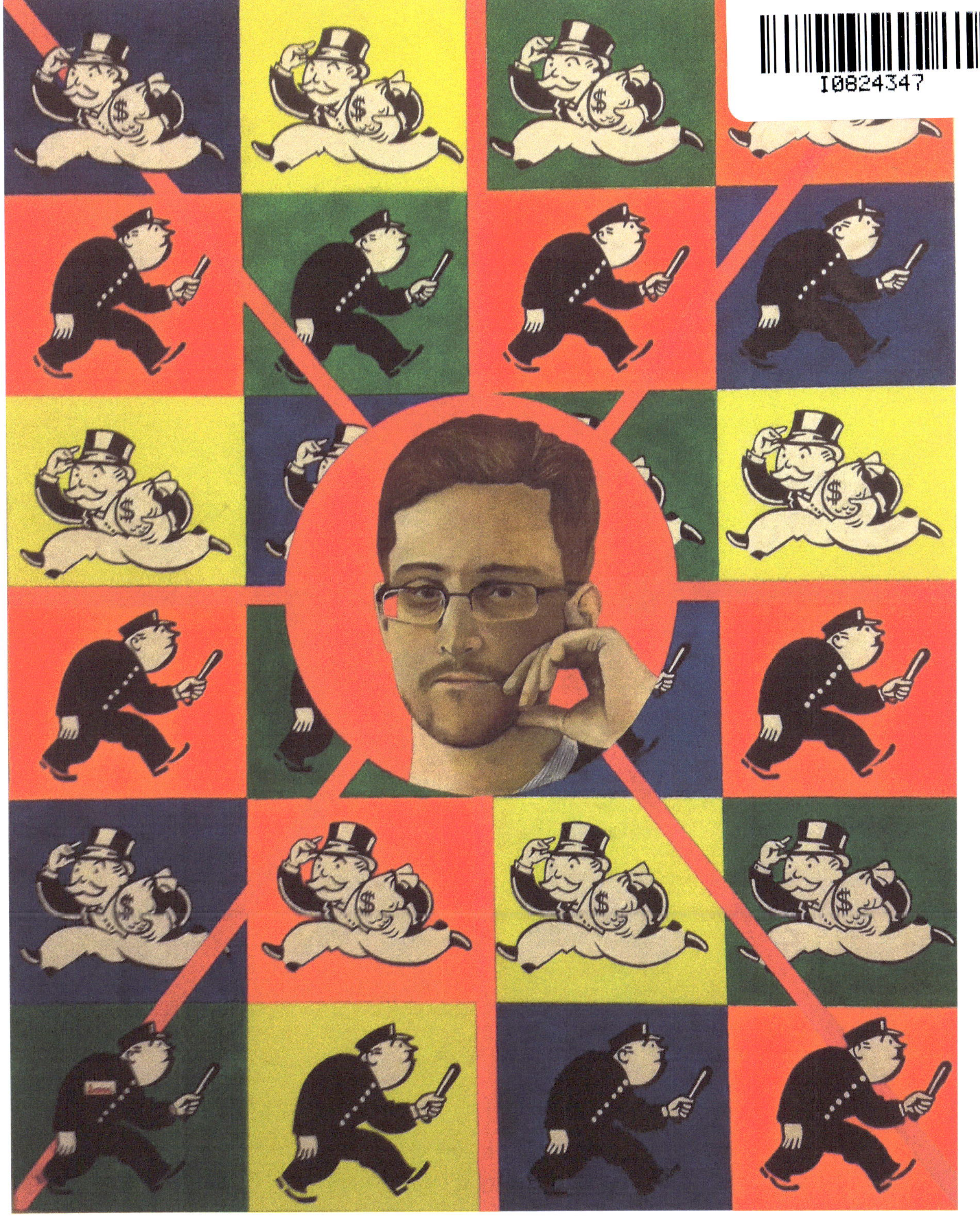

Sensitive Skin Magazine is also available online at
www.sensitiveskinmagazine.com.

Editor-in-Chief: Bernard Meisler
Editors: Rob Hardin, B. Kold
Contributing Editors: Steve Horowitz, Ron Kolm, Tim Beckett and Patrick O'Neil
Thanks to: Franklin Mount

Front cover: *Samoa*
Back cover: from the collection of Mark Michaelson

You can find us at:
Facebook—**www.facebook.com/sensitiveskin**
Twitter—**www.twitter.com/sensitivemag**
YouTube—**www.youtube.com/sensitiveskintv**

We also publish Sensitive Skin Magazine in various electronic formats (Kindle, PDF, etc.), as well as our own lines of books and recordings. For more info about **Sensitive Skin Books**, please go to
www.sensitiveskinmagazine.com/books/
and for **Sensitive Skin Music**, go to
www.sensitiveskinmagazine.com/downloads-store/.

To purchase back issues of this magazine in printed or PDF format, go to
www.sensitiveskinmagazine.com/back-issues/.

You can contact us at **info@sensitiveskinmagazine.com**.

Submissions: **www.sensitiveskinmagazine.com/submissions**.

ISBN-10: 0996157026
ISBN-13: 978-0-9961570-2-5

Contents

Mesrine

Jacques Mesrine (translated by Catherine Texier & Robert Greene)

In late February 1972, all my friends finally ended up in block 2. The winter was harsh. We had more than three feet of snow. Right away, Jean-Paul Mercier became a close friend. We saw eye to eye about everything. I knew he was capable of going to the extreme limit in even the most improbable situation. I knew he was ready to risk the impossible. He worked in the metal shop with Pierre. The equipment was controlled by a guard, sole owner of the keys to the tools' stockroom. Same deal on my side. The winter was bad, but spring brought the melting of snow and some hope.

During a walk, I took Jean-Paul aside:

"Listen, we've got to find some way, even if it means risking our lives. We've got to find a way to get past these damned fences."

"You mean, during the walk?"

"Yes, in full daylight."

"But it's suicidal!"

"We're already fucking dying here already . . . what's the difference?"

"Nothing, you're right. OK, Jacques. Let's give ourselves a deadline; otherwise we'll go insane from thinking too much."

"Before next fall, we're out, or else forget it, deal?"

"Deal."

I smiled at him and shook his hand to seal our commitment.

"Free or dead, even if we rip ourselves up to shreds on the barbed wire."

We were going to keep our promise.

We had noticed during our walks that a few guards would doze in the watchtowers, especially on Monday mornings. We came to the conclusion that they drank too much on Sunday. Over the course of several weeks we studied this human weakness, to check the lapses of attention of the men in charge of watching us. Several times I tossed a tennis ball near the fence and walked across the white line without triggering any reaction from the watchtowers. There was the flaw; it was up to us to exploit it. We noted the names of five such sleepy guards. Jean-Paul was overexcited:

"Can you imagine, Jacques, if two of the five find themselves in the watchtowers one Monday morning? What do you think?"

"We need tools to cut the fences. You work in the metal shop. Up to you to find a solution. Do you think you could swap out triangular files? If you can, get me some iron filings and I'll use them to cover the fake wooden files I'll make for you—guaranteed to be a perfect imitation. Don't forget I used to be model maker . . . . It can come in handy to have once been honest!" I told him with a smile.

"But to get them out of the shop . . . . That's impossible. Neither of us can manage that."

"Neither of us will have to do that. Gauthier will do it."

"You've got to be kidding me! He's the head of security."

"Exactly. He'll never suspect what I'm cooking up. This is what I'm thinking. We're the ones making the wooden tennis rackets. All we'll have to do is to break a few of them and ask to have them replaced. I'll make them myself and I'll insert the files into the handles. Since the shop foreman will give the rackets to Gauthier, he's the one who'll give them to us in the courtyard. If he runs them through the metal detector, we're screwed; but I am positive he won't do it. How could he possibly think of something like that?"

Jean-Paul laughed his ass off.

"Yes! Yesss! That one takes the cake! To get out of here with the complicity of the head of security! Ok, Jacques, I'll do what I can with the files."

Little by little our plan took shape. I told all our friends what we were up to because we needed the full complicity of both shops to complete the first part. Everything went as planned.

On August 21, 1972, we went out in the yard for our walk. My friends took their positions to watch whether the guards were paying attention to us. Each move that they made looked natural but signaled a code that meant something to me. One guard was standing outside the fences on our right, his dog sitting at his feet. He was armed with a .12-caliber pump-action shotgun filled with buckshot. He was talking with the guard in the watchtower on the right, who, as a result, had his back to us. The guard in the watchtower on the left was dozing off. I placed our chessboard on the roller that was used to smooth out the tennis court. I had been doing this regularly for a month to get the guards used to seeing us play in that spot. Two of my friends were facing me. Jean-Paul was squatting behind them. We were against the wall, only fifteen feet away from the fence on the left. Lafleur was sitting on the sandpit, which was located across from the watchtower on the left, pretending to read. Another friend was doing gymnastic exercises across from the watchtower on the right; his moves could become coded signals in case of danger. I glanced around the yard. Everything was OK.

"Now! Go!"

Jean-Paul nimbly crossed the white line and stretched out on the ground, face against the fence. He was totally motionless. His green-colored clothes blended with the grass. No reaction from the watchtowers. The man with the dog was still talking. Jean-Paul was supposed to cut only when I told him to. He was my hands, I was his eyes. The slightest mistake and it was all over.

"Go ahead, cut!"

With his triangular file, he severed one link after another, moving upward. In ten minutes the passage was big enough to let one man pass. I saw him slip through the barbed wire between the two fences. If even one of the guards noticed him, he was dead, sure to be shot down on the spot. But he coolly made his way out. The moment he was about to start working on the second fence, I heard the patrol car coming.

"Don't move. Not one move."

The car followed the road that encircled the whole walk on the outside. Jean-Paul saw the tires pass four feet from his face. The car drove on and stopped in front of the watchtower on the left. If, by some misfortune, one of the guards from the patrol car got out with the dog that accompanied them, anything could happen. The man in the watchtower leaned forward to greet the driver. Our nerves were shot; we were so close to the goal! When the car drove on, I waited for a moment, then told Jean-Paul:

"All right, keep going."

He went back to work as cool as a cucumber. Then I saw him crawl outside. He had managed to pass through to the other side. Body glued against the fence, he told me:

"Your turn, Frenchie."

My friends created a diversion. I, too, crawled through both openings. I only had one thought: I was going to be free. We had agreed that we would leave two by two. The first departure belonged to us by right. We had taken all the risks, and they were huge. Indeed, if we were spotted, it was certain death—we'd be shot down like dogs by vindictive guards. But it would be the death of a free man, a man who has made his choice. I felt no fear—my moves were guided only by a great determination.

I found myself lying down next to Jean-Paul. Our hands met. They sealed a bond between us that would never be broken. Until his death, three years later, shot down by the Montreal police.

We had to cross the road. Our clothes risked standing out against its light color. A new diversion was created when I made a sign. I could see my friends who were still prisoners, those who had believed in our plan and those who had always doubted. I promised myself not to forget them and to keep my promise to attack this penitentiary to try to free them all.

By quickly rolling our bodies across the road, we reached the ditch. The grass was high, and we blended in with the surrounding green. Our backs to the watchtower, we began to crawl. I got a glimpse of the third watchtower, which was catty-cornered to the entrance. I visualized the look on Gauthier's mug and couldn't help smiling. We had to crawl for another three hundred feet until we reached a thicket where we could finally get up without being seen. Jean-Paul gave me a friendly tap on the head.

"We made it, Frenchie. Can you believe it, we're free!"

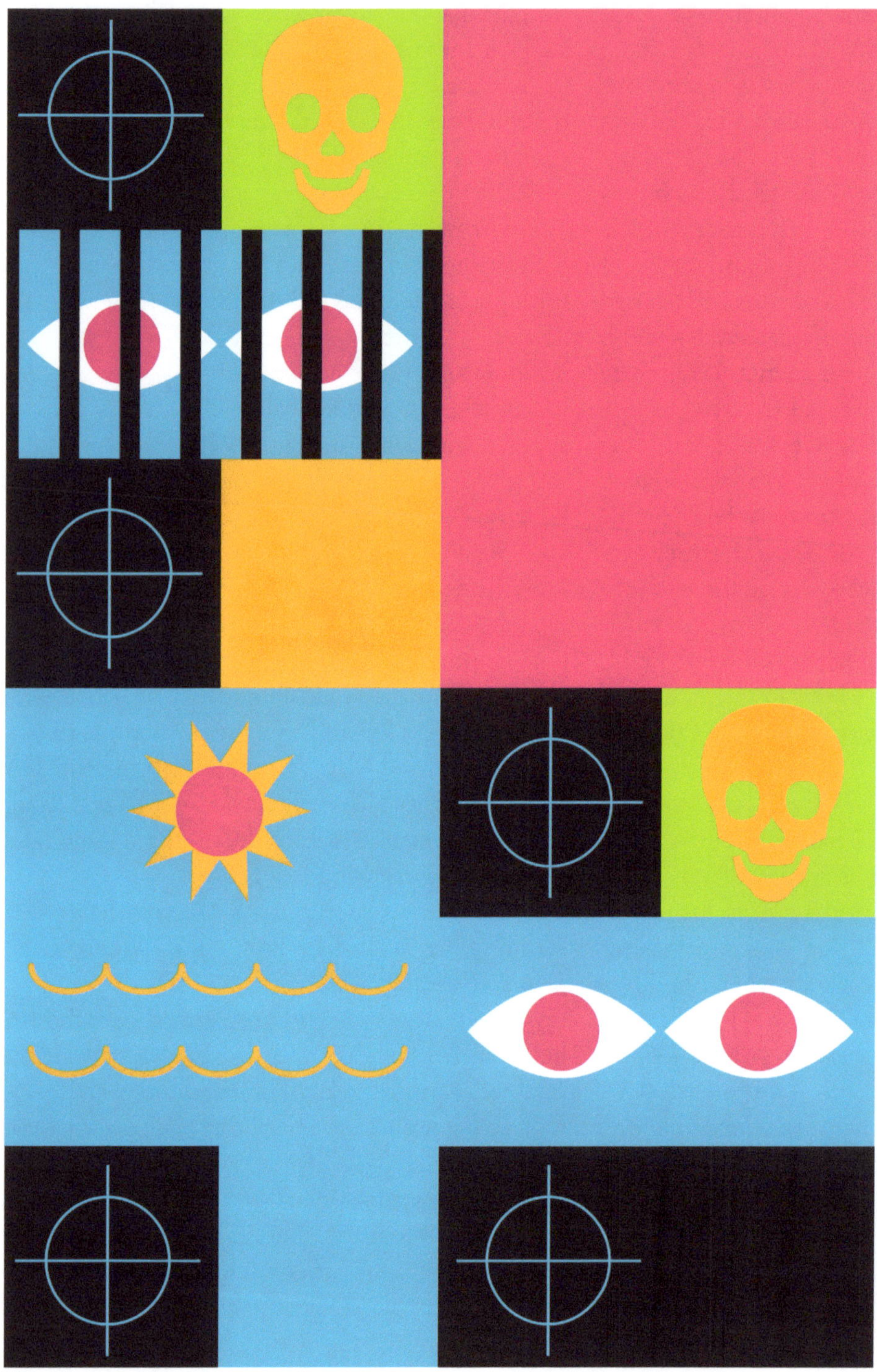

Illustration by JD King

"Let's hurry, kiddo...we need a car."

I could see the penitentiary through the trees. This man-eater hadn't devoured me. The men were walking around the courtyard as though nothing had happened. Everything was quiet. The next departure would take place in a few minutes. Lafleur, Pierre Vincent, then Imbeau and Ouillet, and the others if they could.

We started to run. The trees protected us all the way to the highway, which we crossed to reach a little wood. A creek ran through it; we crossed it. We had been gone from the prison for more than fifteen minutes now, but we were still in the danger zone. At the moment we were about to exit the woods we heard a helicopter. We threw ourselves to the ground.

"Fuck, they already sounded the alarm," I said.

"No, look, it's flying over the highway, it's one of those copters that give traffic info to the truck drivers. Damn, that scared the shit out of us!"

He was right, the copter was flying away.

In the distance, peasants were working in the fields. We waved at them, and they casually waved back. We got to a crossroad. At that moment, a car occupied by two men slowed down to make the turn. I rushed to the back door and got into the vehicle, to the men's great surprise. Jean-Paul did the same on the other side.

The driver tried to protest: "Hey! What are you doing?"

The answer came, dry and threatening:

"Shut the fuck up. We just escaped from the SCU. You do as we say or you're dead. Your choice."

The simple word SCU was synonymous with "killer" for all the people in the area. The driver was freaking out. I quickly reassured him:

"Just drive us to Montreal, that's all."

His friend, who was much calmer, made him understand that it was best to follow my orders, so we took the highway. I forced the driver's companion to open the glove compartment to make sure there were no weapons in it. Jean-Paul searched it and emptied the guy's pockets. He didn't say anything. He seemed to be amused by the situation. With a humorous tone, I told him:

"I'm just borrowing a few dollars from you for the phone. You can ask the SCU to pay you back. I wouldn't want you to think I'm a thief!"

And I gave him back the rest of his money.

We got close to Montreal. The alarm had certainly been sounded. We still had to go over a bridge; maybe they had set up a roadblock.

"Pull over here."

"But . . ."

"I said, stop here."

He stopped the car.

"You and your friend, get out of the car. Things might get pretty hot in a little while. We'll go on without you, unless you want to get shot at, if the police are waiting for us at the bridge."

His friend told him to do as we said. Physically, neither of them was strong enough to confront us.

Jean-Paul quickly got behind the wheel and we took off, leaving the men on the side of the road. There was no roadblock waiting for us. Once we got to town I rushed to a phone booth. I immediately called Lizon, the name of a woman Pierre told us to contact.

"Hi Lizon? I'm a friend of Pierre's. We made it. Quick, come get us."

I told her where we were.

"I'll be there in fifteen minutes."

Jean-Paul parked the car in a parking lot and came back to join me. We removed our shirts to be in our undershirts. With our pants dirty with soil, we could easily pass for construction workers, but certainly not for escapees on the lam.

We had to wait for Lizon, so we walked into a little restaurant and—relaxed as can be—we ordered our first coffee as free men. The young woman at the counter was listening to her transistor radio with the volume turned low. It had been forty-five minutes since we had left the SCU. On the radio, we were startled to hear the news release.

"Warning . . . warning . . . police news release. There has been a breakout from the high security center. Six dangerous criminals have escaped. These men are extremely dangerous and might be armed. If you see them, do not try to stop them. Contact the Laval police precinct. Once again, these men are dangerous. We will give you more information as soon as it's available."

And the music came back on. Jean-Paul looked at me, like, "Six . . . not bad, hey, Frenchie?"

I smiled at him. The girl behind the counter said to her girlfriend:

"They must be far away. Hope they don't catch them!"

I felt like telling her that we couldn't be any closer and to thank her for her good wishes, but I pretended not to have any interest in the information.

According to the restaurant clock, fifteen minutes had passed. I got out first. I recognized her immediately from Pierre's description. I nodded to her. She nodded back and walked toward a car. I climbed in the front and Jean-Paul in the back.

"Hey guys," she said. "What about Pierrot?"

"Out and about... If everything works well, he should join us soon."

"There's everything you'll need in the duffel bag."

The two .38 specials and a sawed-off M1 rifle, along with three cartridge clips with twenty-five bullets each, were welcome. There were also several bright-colored shirts. We each put one on. I looked at Jean-Paul with satisfaction:

"Now, kiddo, we're truly free."

An excerpt from Mesrine, *the autobiography of Jacques Mesrine, translated from the French to English by Catherine Texier and Robert Greene (TamTam Books).*

Four Poems

Hal Sirowitz

Removing Her Boots

She took off
her boots and
said now she can
get down and dirty.
She got down
but before she
could get dirty,
she fell asleep.

Petting

She took me
to the petting zoo.
The only bad thing
was I had to wait
in line with all
the other animals.

Simple Simon

If Simple Simon was really so simple,
Father said, how come he became
the hero of a nursery game.
I haven't heard anyone shouting
out your name, yet. Maybe you should try
to act simple and see where it gets you.
Acting complex has gotten you nowhere fast.
You've become an authority on nothingness,
able to find it on any map. It's where
the highway never goes.

The Adult Version

Jack and Jill ran up the hill
to have sex. Then, they decided
it was the wrong place—too out
in the open. So Jack fetched a pail
of water, hoping during the descent
he could think of a suitable place.
That was when he fell, because
he wasn't concentrating on the pail.
And that Jill came tumbling down
after Jack proved that she was
thinking about sex, too.

Horse Track Portraits

Justin Clifford Rhody

I've been working on the Horse Track Portrait series almost every Sunday for three years now at the Golden Gate Fields horse track in Berkeley. All the photos are of anonymous people at the edge of the track fence during the brief races and were shot without the subject's knowledge/consent. I'm in the very early stages of editing this material into a book and hope to have a dummy compiled this fall. I usually preface the slide-show presentations of this work with a quote from Frederick Sommers: "Only chance is fair."

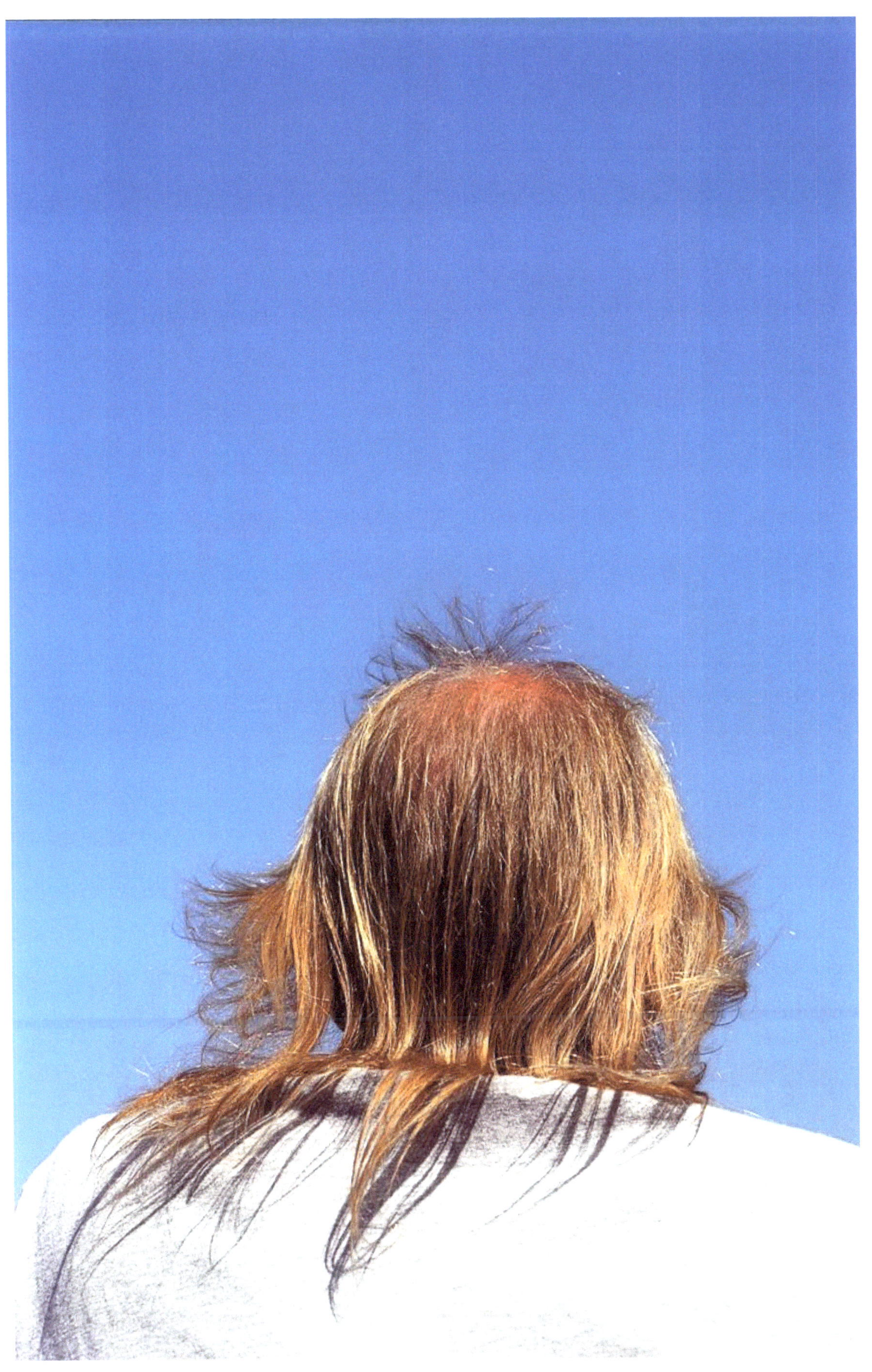

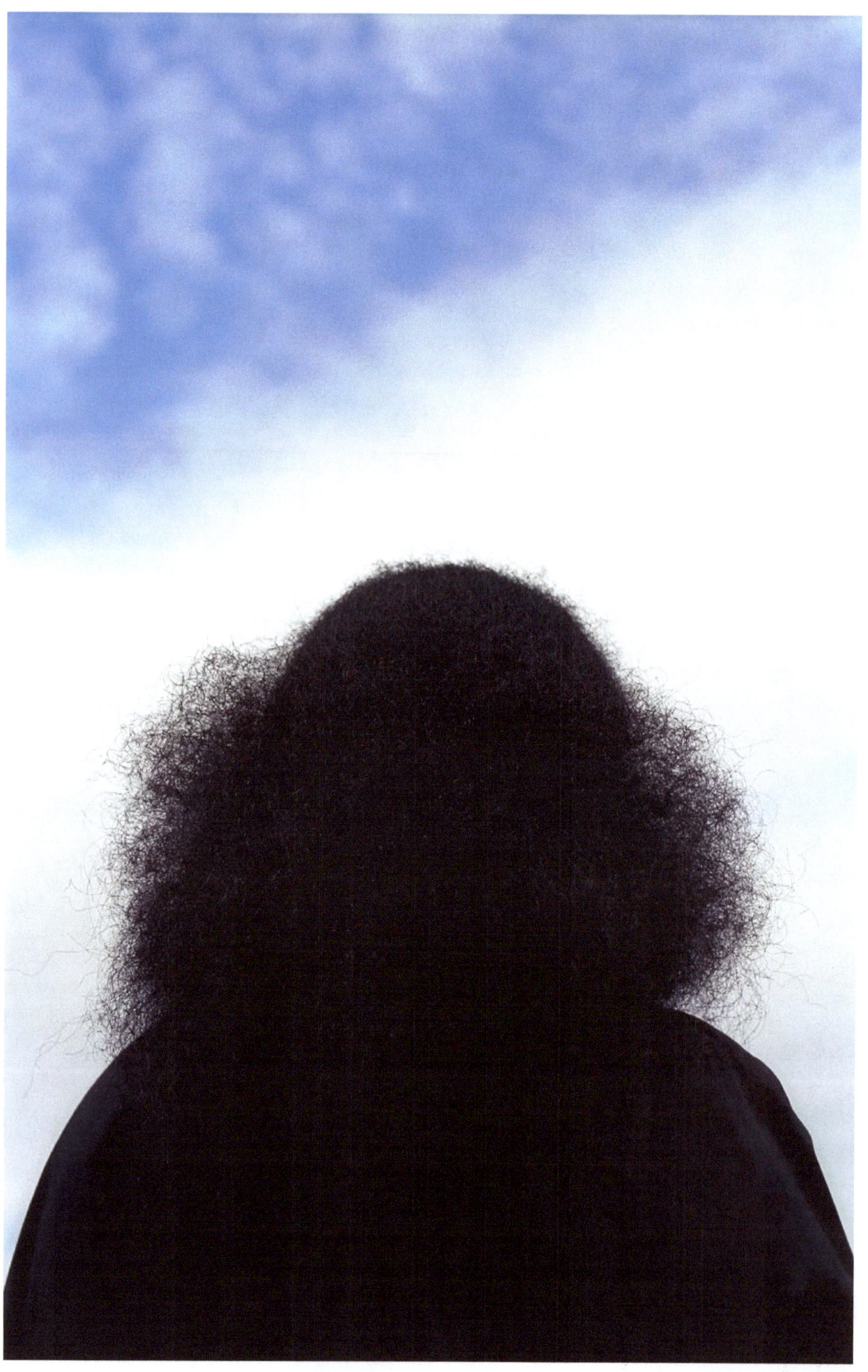

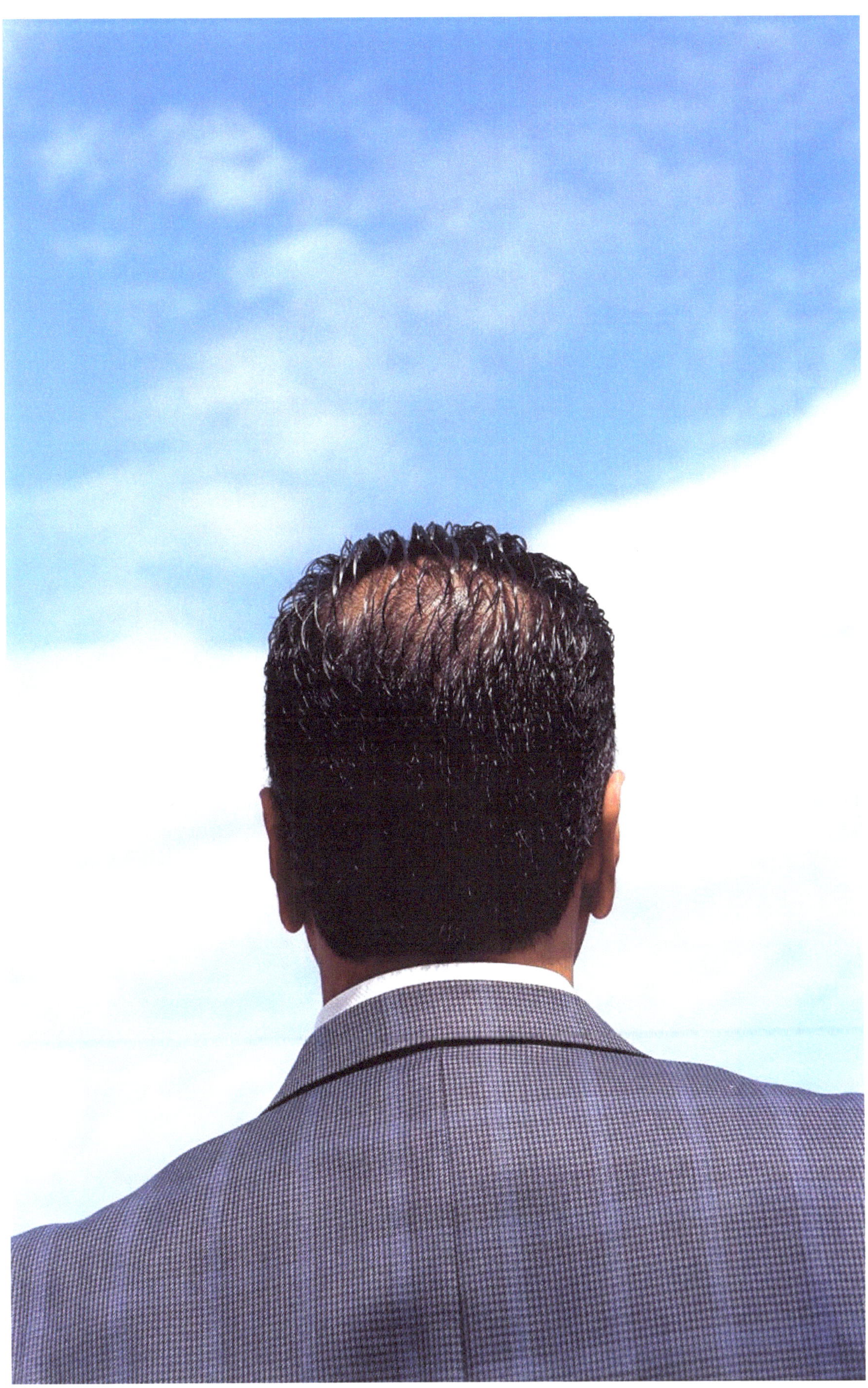

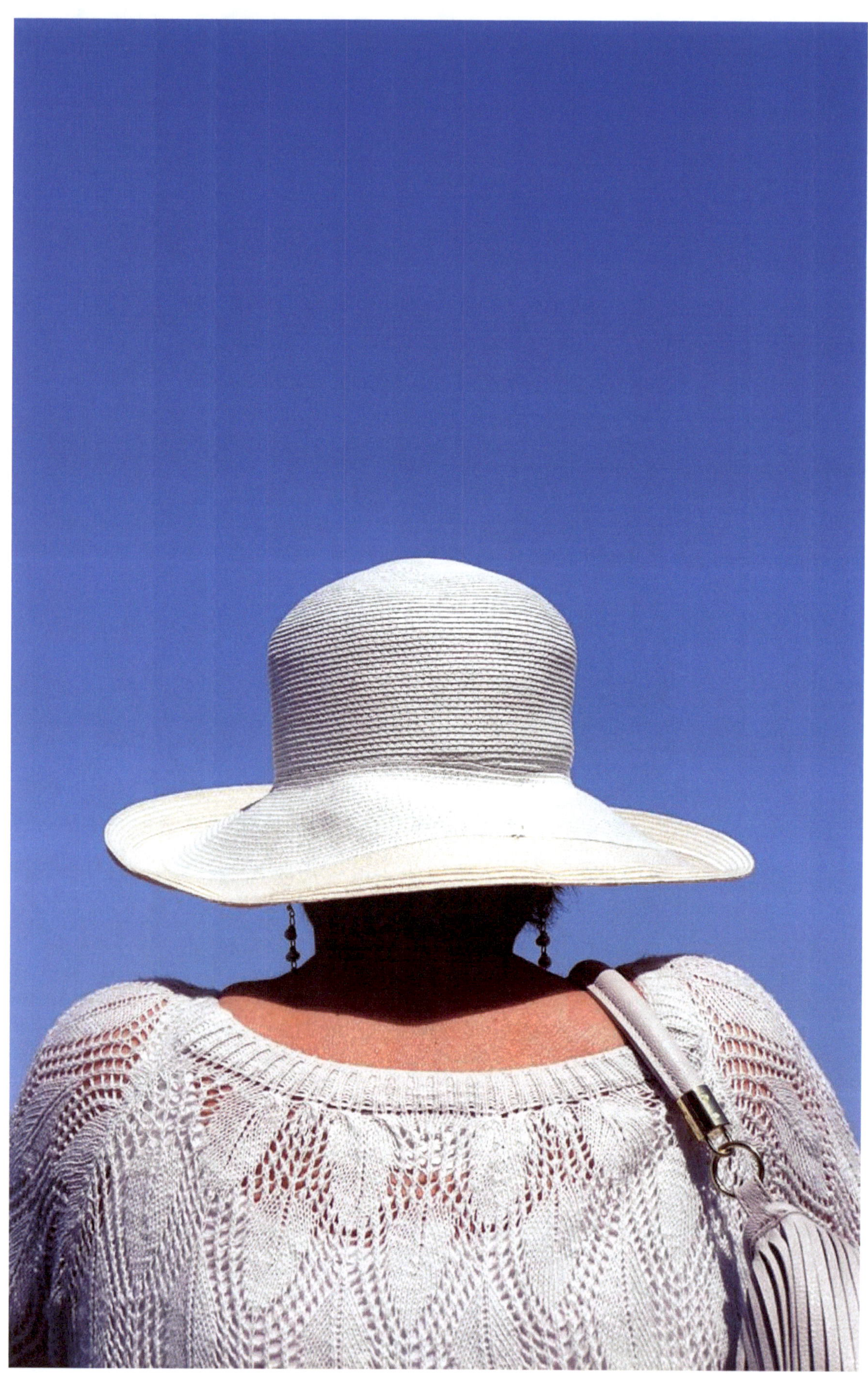

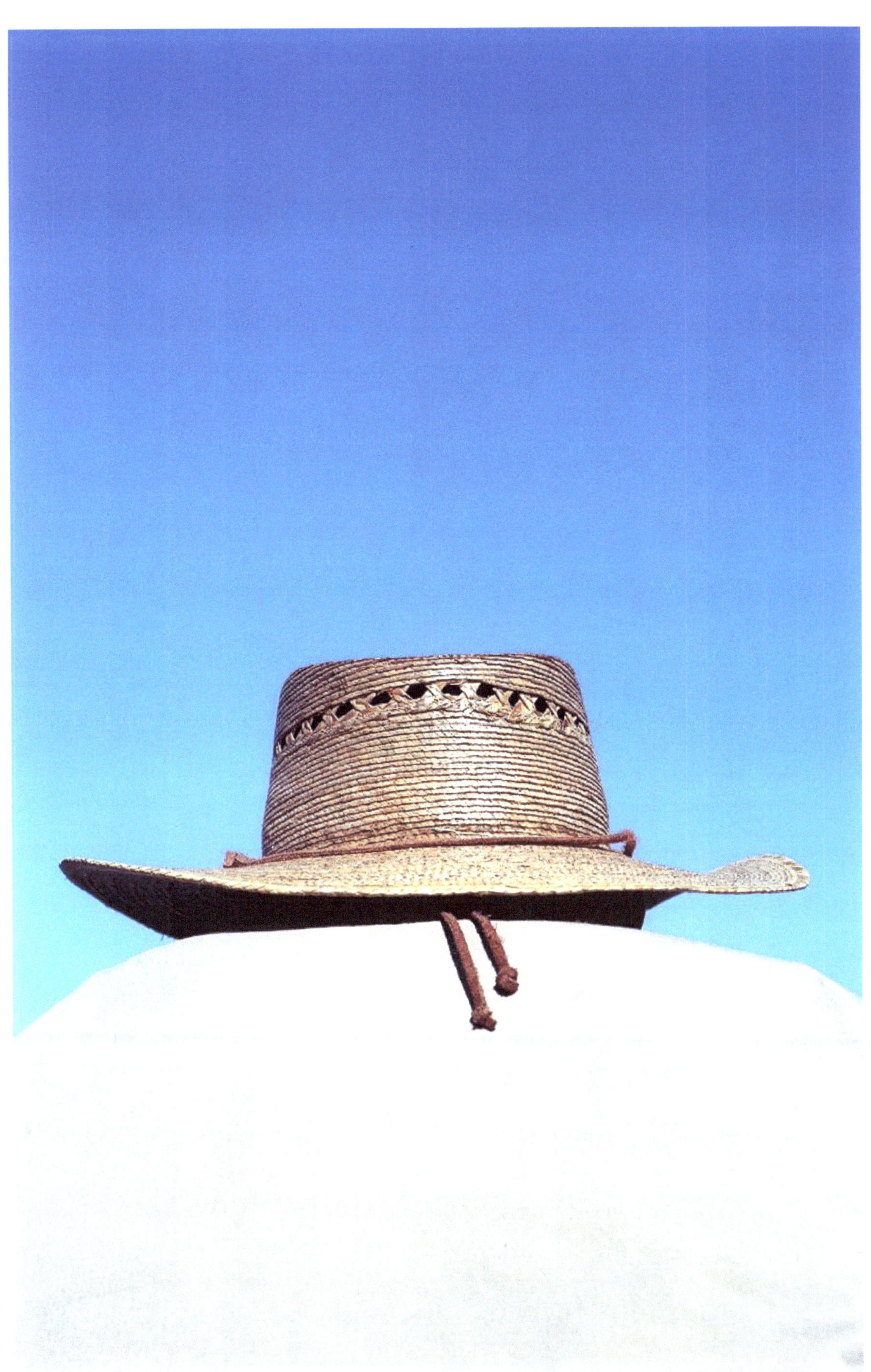

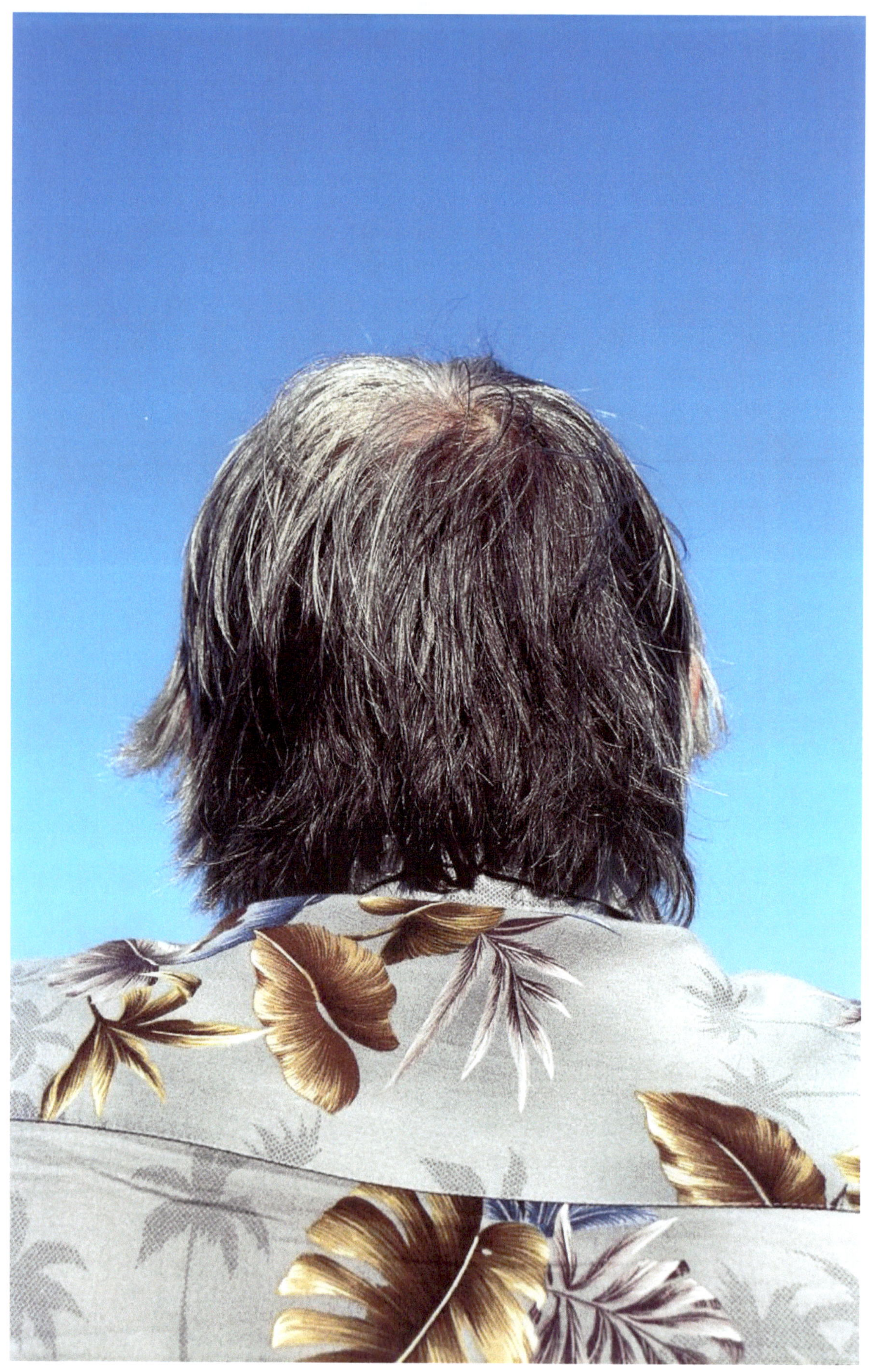

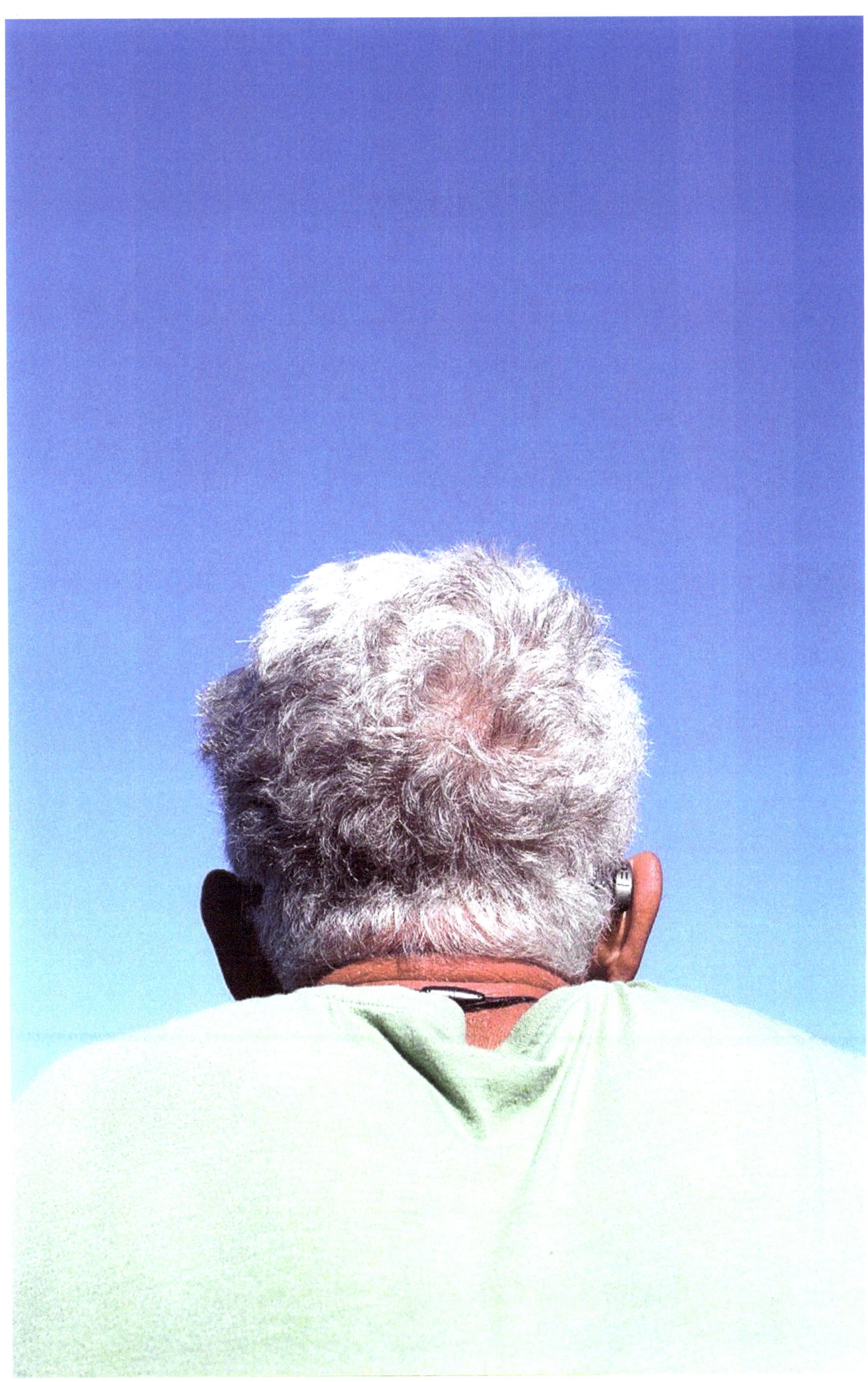

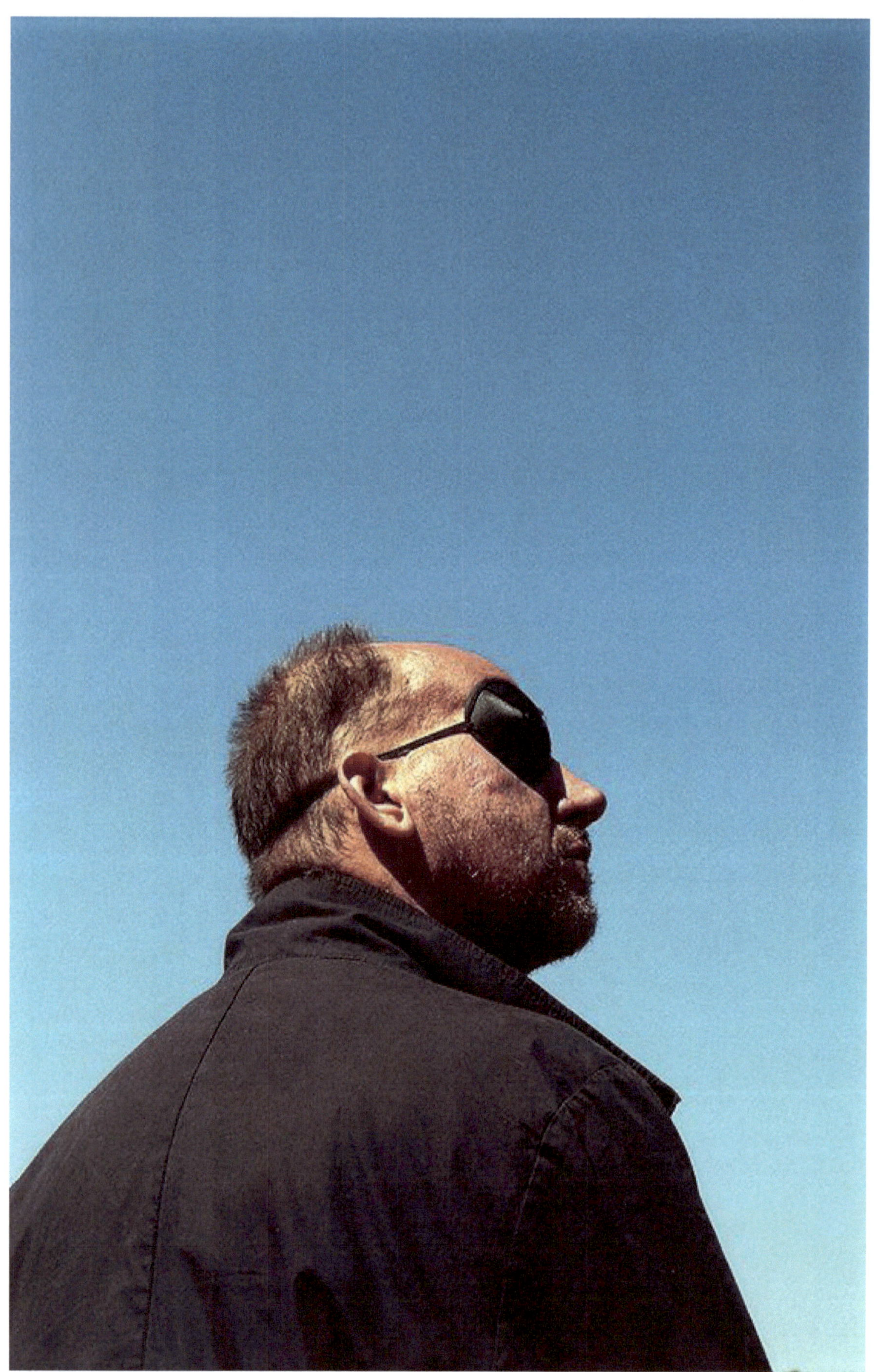

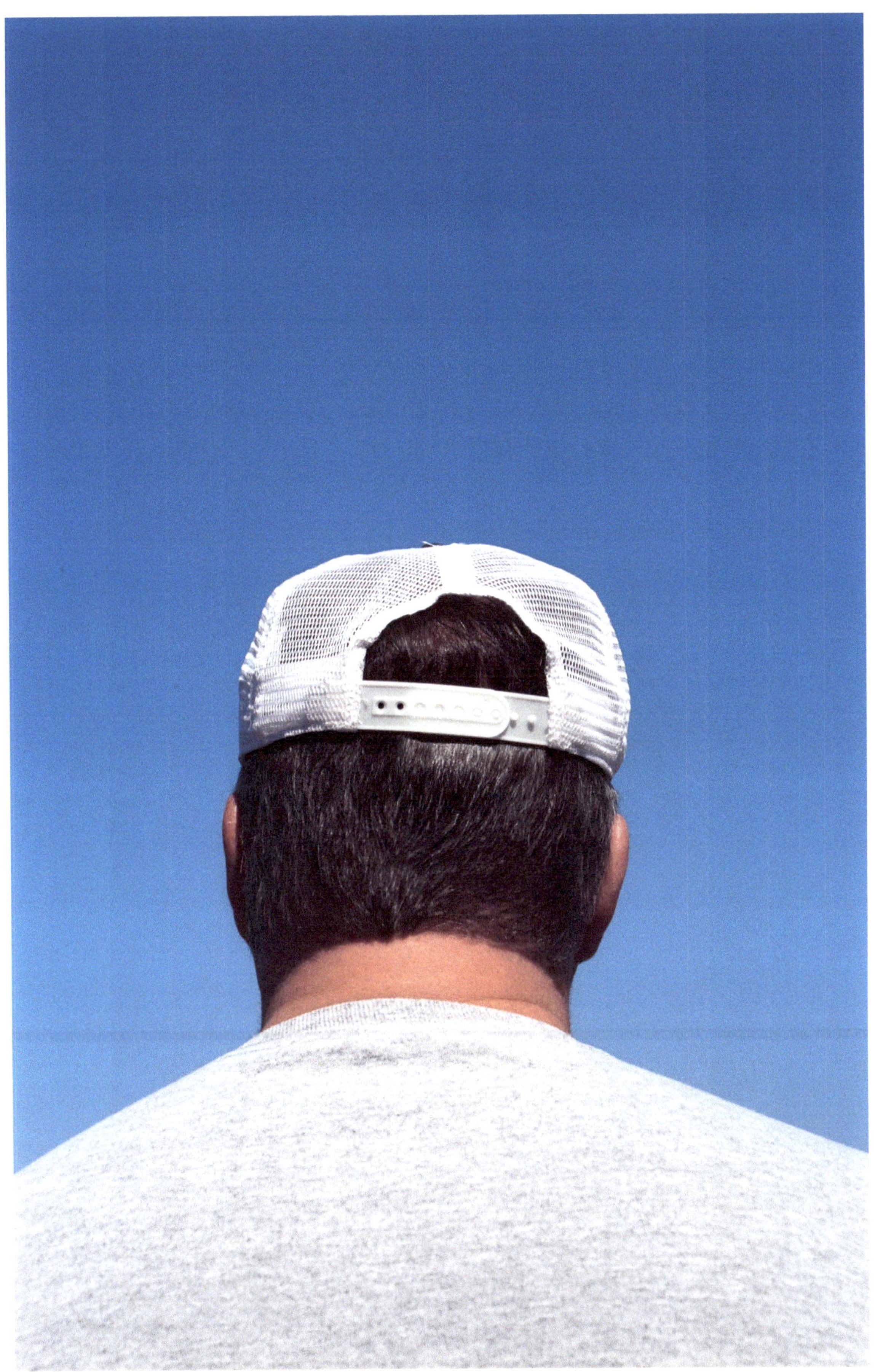

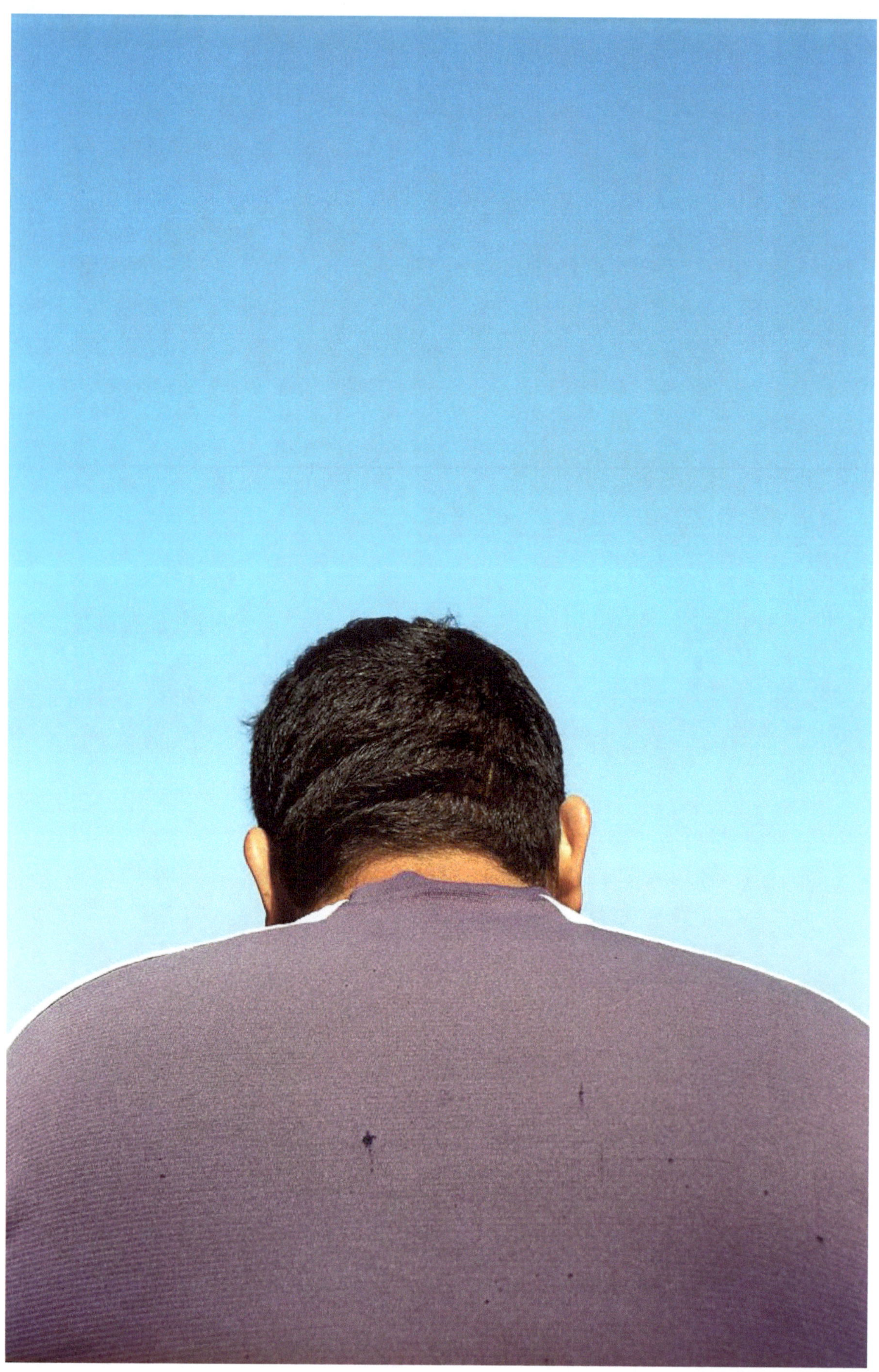

The Storm

Peter Blauner

He liked to have his house in order, which was why he'd never had a family or pets. He liked his routines and there was nothing wrong with that. Every day in the summer months, he wore his father's old Fire Department windbreaker, with a blue FDNY polo shirt, khaki shorts and flip-flops, so he could walk down to the beach without getting a chill from the ocean. When the weather turned, he had a half-dozen identical blue sweatshirts that he wore with velour track pants and thick wool socks for going out on the deck. Fortunately, he only had to go out once a week for groceries at the Stop & Shop on Rockaway Beach Boulevard, because the settlement he got from the city after the accident let him stay home and mind his business. So naturally he wasn't going to open the door for a stranger in the middle of a storm.

The doorbell started ringing just after the first commercial break for the Cheers rerun. He didn't like sports or these new shows with singing and dancing contests, where crazy people screamed with joy and disappointment and there was no telling how things would end up. It was much better when you could anticipate and prepare yourself beforehand. Which was why he'd been paying attention to the weather reports. He had the generator running and the storm windows latched tight with foam and sealing tape around the edges. It gave him a secure feeling when he heard the first few drops on the glass like the claws of hungry little animals that would eventually give up and go look for shelter somewhere else. But then the bell started.

> *...he could hear the wind howling and feel the storm trying to get in the house. He went to the door and looked out the peephole. Three hooded figures were on his front porch, like something from a nightmare or a Lord of the Rings movie.*

It was a soft modulated two-tone, the sound of the same bell his parents had put in when they bought the house on stilts in 1970. He liked that sound because it didn't disturb him too much when he had to get up for a delivery.

He ignored the bell the first time it rang because it was after nine o'clock and who would be out on a night like this? It went off a second time a half-minute later and he reached for the remote to turn the sound up. All his life he'd lived in Rockaway, maintaining his parents' house just the way they'd had it—plus painting the shingles every four years and putting in fiberglass insulation and a new alarm system—while the rest of the neighborhood was going to hell with those people from the projects and the ocean was getting filthy. He could count on less than one hand the times a stranger had come to his door for a legitimate reason. Ten seconds later, the bell went off for a third time. It felt like someone poking a dirty fingernail in his ear over and over.

He crossed his arms and ankles, and made himself all tight and tense as he leaned back in the

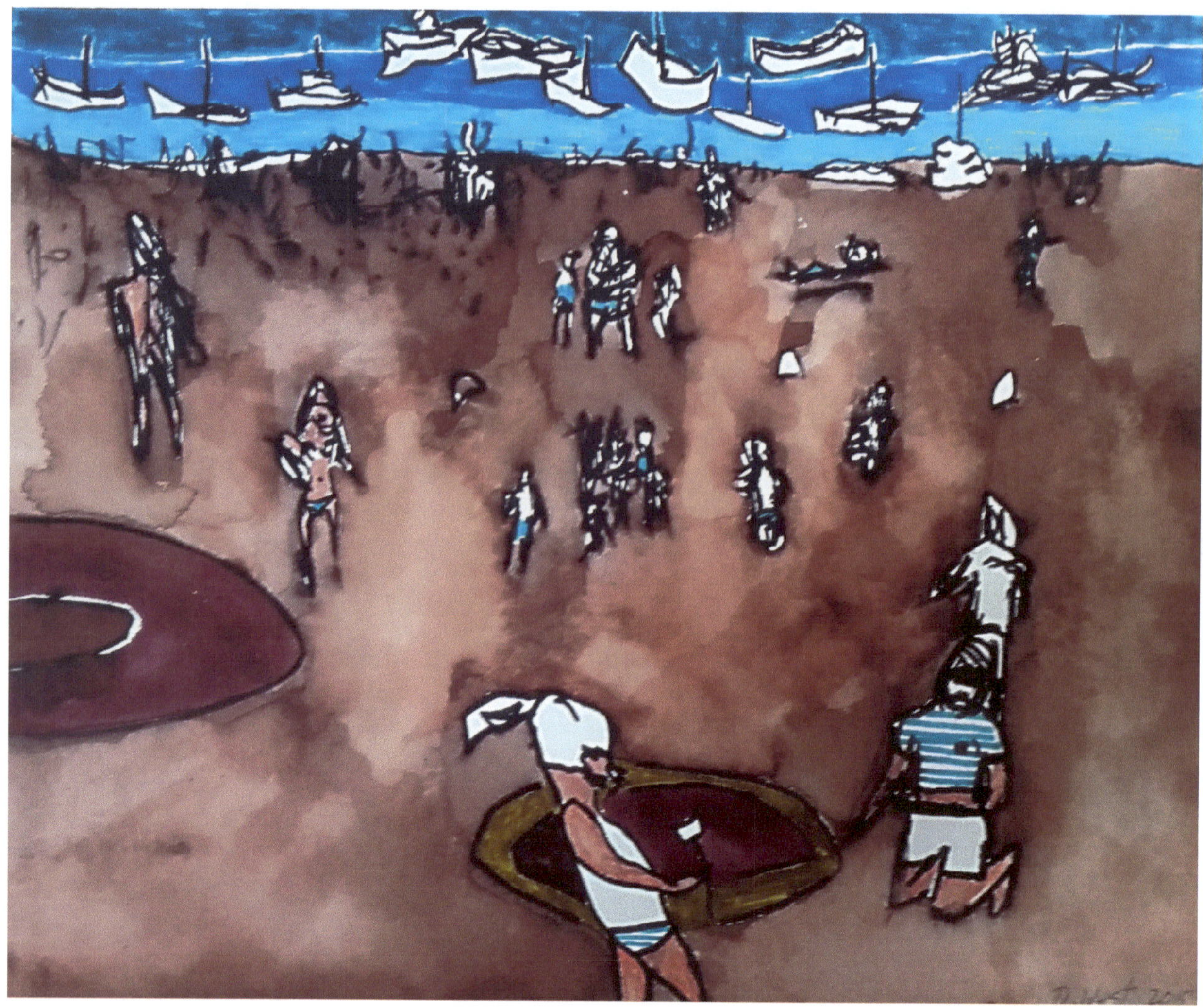

La Plage á St. Lunaire, ink, cochineal and naugalina on paper, 2015, David West

Barcalounger, wishing they'd just go away. But of course, they didn't. The bell started ringing more frantically, so that he couldn't hear his show, couldn't think about anything except to ask himself the question, why wouldn't people just leave him alone? He realized he was going to have to get up or else this would be going on all night.

As soon as he stood, he could hear the wind howling and feel the storm trying to get in the house. He went to the door and looked out the peephole. Three hooded figures were on his front porch, like something from a nightmare or a Lord of the Rings movie. Ghoul-wraiths of unequal size in silhouette, with curtains of wild monsoon rain moving back and forth across the sidewalk behind them. Just seeing them put the dampness in his bones.

"Hello," a high ragged voice called out. "Can you please help us?"

He kept his eye at the peephole and blinked, glad they couldn't see him.

"I'm sorry to bother you. But your house is the only one that has a light on the block. All the others are dark."

The ghoul to the right of the speaker went into a squat. The other leaned on one of the porch columns and sucked its thumb.

"Our car has stalled and the streets are flooding. We're just trying to get to my sister's in Brooklyn."

When he didn't answer, the speaker suddenly

reached out and banged on the door with the brass knocker. It had been years since anyone used it and he jumped back, almost slipping on his mother's old throw rug. From the living room, he could hear the laughter from the *Cheers* audience, reminding him of the warmth and comfort he'd left behind. His tea and cell phone were on the coffee table. He knew it would useless to try to call 911. With the way the government had been whipping people up about this hurricane, he knew the police and fire department would never come. He was alone and unprotected.

"We only need to come inside for a while. It's not safe out here."

It was a black woman's voice. He was sure of that now. With a slight Caribbean lilt when she said "Brooklyn." This was how it started. Sometimes they pretended to be emergency workers from Con Ed or the gas company, coming to check on the lines. Why wouldn't they send a woman with small children up to some trusting idiot's door?

He should have kept pestering his brother, the big macho state trooper, to help him get a gun a few years ago, instead of letting the subject drop when it was suggested that he could just drive to Florida or some place like that and buy one himself with just a driver's license.

"Go away," he yelled.

It was the awful how his voice cracked when he was nervous and made him sound like his mother. He should have kept pestering his brother, the big macho state trooper, to help him get a gun a few years ago, instead of letting the subject drop when it was suggested that he could just drive to Florida or some place like that and buy one himself with a driver's license. Obviously, that wasn't going to happen. But now he was here by himself, defenseless, with these creatures at his door, demanding to be let in.

"Mister, it's dark out here. My children are shivering. Cars are getting carried away by the water. We just need to be inside."

He saw the one that was crouching hang its head and sniffle. He pictured this wet little urchin curled up on his sofa, coughing and spewing bacteria on the cushions.

"I can't," he said. "I'm sorry."

"What'd he tell you, mom?" the thumb-sucker asked.

"I know you're a good person, sir." The woman pushed her body against his door. "I know you want to help us."

He could hear her clothes squish. All of them sodden. Dying to come into his house, to soak the carpets and use the bathrooms. The little ones would probably miss the toilet and piss on the fluffy white rugs. They'd blow their noses on the good towels, and use the nice soap, and then they'd be hungry and thirsty and he'd have to stand there and watch them drink his orange juice straight out of the container. They'd go into his bedroom and look through his closets for dry clothes. Then they'd want to come downstairs, and the little ones would want to sit in his Barcalounger, and use the remote to change the channel and watch their own programs. And their mother would want to talk. She'd want to tell him about all the misery in her life that had led her to being alone on a street where she didn't belong, with two children in the middle of a hurricane, and he'd be expected to nod, listen and say the right things without wanting to scream and jump out of his skin. Then she'd yawn, and smile, and put her hand on top of his, and ask if it would be all right if they just stayed until the storm passed and the sun came up. After that, he knew he would never be able to get rid of them.

"You're not coming in my house," he said.

He stepped back from the peephole, clenching his jaw and bracing himself against the door in case she hit it again or had her children start crying. He could hear the wind getting fiercer now, pelting the rain harder against the side of his house and ripping away part of the awning over the front door. He could hear it go flapping off like a wounded vulture, while his garbage cans rolled down the street and sirens wailed in the far distance, as cops and paramedics attended to other people's emergencies.

The news van showed up on the block two days later. There was still water in the street, not just from the storm but from the fire truck hoses that had spewed in vain from the dozens of houses around him that had burned down.

From the living room, the *Cheers* crowd was enjoying being in a friendly place where everybody knows your name. He stood in the foyer for a few more seconds, not daring to move in case she heard him and called out again. But now the only sound was the yowling of natural forces tearing at the boardwalk and sluicing water into the streets. So he went back to his show and told himself that none of this had really happened or mattered.

The news van showed up on the block two days later. There was still water in the street, not just from the storm but also the fire truck hoses that had spewed the dozens of houses around him in vain, since they'd still burned down. There were cars turned over on lawns, refrigerators, planks from the boardwalk, and large fallen trees blocking every other side street and showing their roots obscenely.

A man with gray hair wearing a news team windbreaker stood in front of his house with a microphone and a camera trained on the front door. He came out and told them to go away. They were trespassing. The newsman replied they were on a public street doing a story about a woman who'd lost her daughters on the corner during the storm. Supposedly they were swept out of her arms during the deluge and had been found dead a half-mile down the road. A six-year-old and a three-year-old, drowned within a few feet of each other. Their mother said a man who lived in this house had refused them shelter a few seconds before she lost them.

Well, of course, that was a damn lie. What was she doing out on a night like that anyway? He'd heard no one. It was just another smear. Spread by those animals who'd already ruined the rest of the neighborhood. Why wouldn't they leave a man in peace? And even if what they said was true, it wasn't against the law—was it? Everyone has a right to be left alone. Anyway, that was all he had to say. Then he went back inside to watch a *M*A*S*H* rerun. A show about people who knew how to laugh and take care of each other in troubled times. They used to make those kinds of shows so well. What happened?

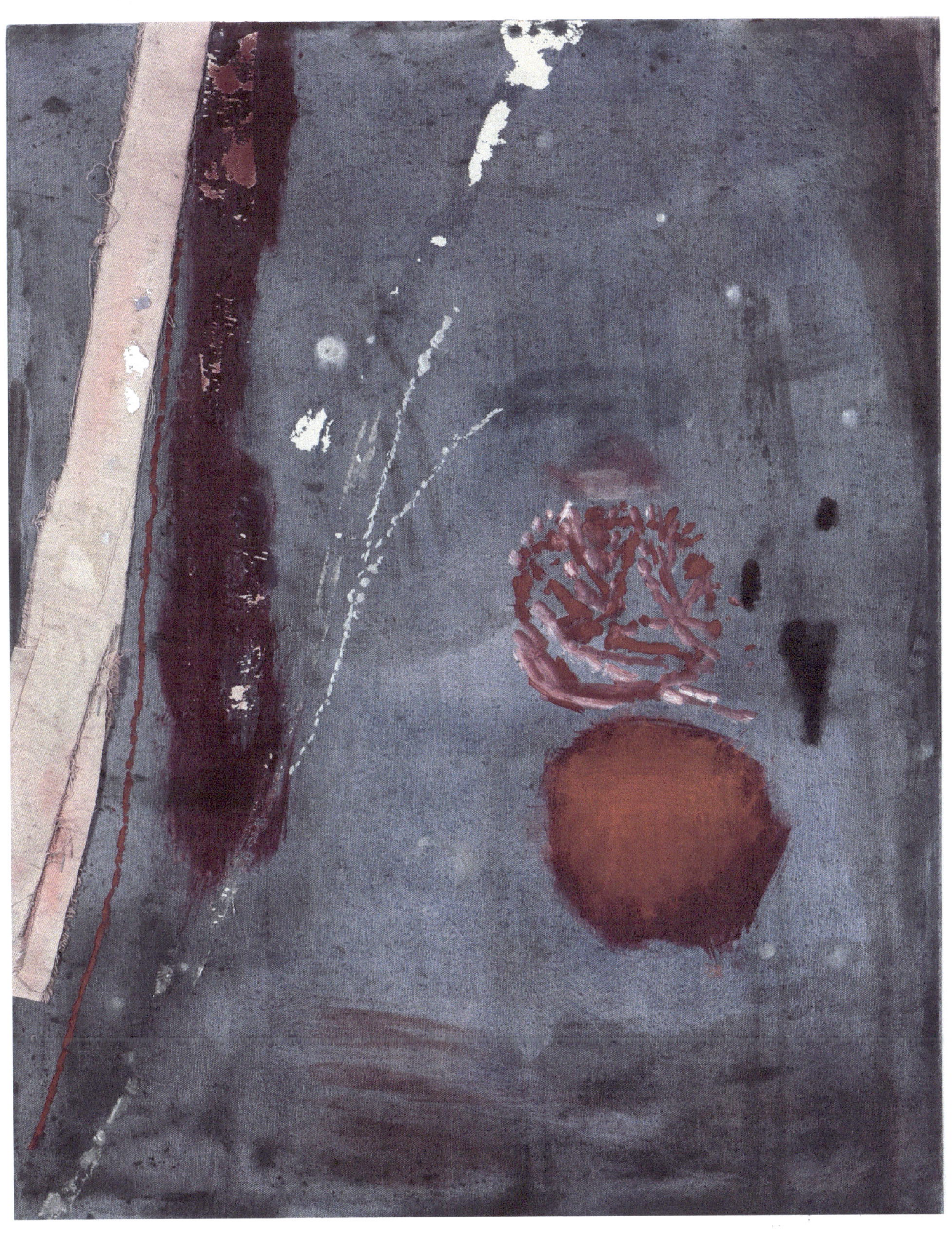

Pine trees, mixed media on canvas, 30" x 22" , 2015, Sally Egbert

Code of Violence

Thaddeus Rutkowski

On the subway, I see a boy who is about 10 years old; he's with his father. Both of them have red hair, but the boy has Asian features—a round face and pointy eyes. His father has a long face and Western eyes. Maybe this boy is something like me, a halfling.

"Do CIA agents use switchblades?" the boy asks his father.

The father makes no reply, and the boy says, "I think they carry hidden knives."

The boy continues, "There was a gun called Hitler's Buzz Saw. It fired three shots per second."

Again, the father doesn't respond.

"Are there still people with Ebola in Texas?" the boy asks. "Why don't they just make them drink poison? That would get rid of them."

"Let's move to the back," the father says, and the two of them head for the seats above the bus's engine.

"Can you believe Hitler's Buzz Saw was that fast?" the boy asks.

I wonder if this is a typical boy, or if he resembles the young Adolf Eichmann. Is this boy a killer in the making? Or is he just a normal kid?

He looks like a normal kid.

> *They are stumbling as they walk; they are off balance. I look at one of them in the eye as I pass; then I look away. He reaches out with the arm closer to me and strikes the side of my head with an open hand.*

*

After I get off the bus, I walk between buildings that house faculty for the local university. The well-lit street is lined with trees. Two young men are walking toward me. Perhaps they are students, going to meet a professor.

They are stumbling as they walk; they are off balance. I look one of them in the eye as I pass; then I look away. He reaches out with the arm closer to me and strikes the side of my head with an open hand.

"Hey!" I say. "Why did you do that?"

He comes at me with both arms hanging, gorilla-like, in front of him. At that point, his friend—if he is a friend—steps in and hugs the aggressor, pinning his arms at his sides. The first man struggles, says, "Let me at him."

"Leave him alone," the supposed friend says.

I hold my hand to the side of my head as I walk by.

*

I arrive at a club to have dinner with a friend of mine. It's the kind of place I'd never visit on my own, but I've been invited. Inside, men wear jackets. My friend takes off his jacket to go to the rest room, and I take off my jacket, too, but I don't leave the table. A wait staffer comes over almost immediately and tells me to put my jacket back on. "You have to wear it at all times," she says, "but we'll make it cooler here for you."

I suppose she is going to adjust the air conditioning in our corner of the room. As time passes, however, I feel no more comfortable than I did.

I tell my friend about the head-slapping incident.

"You were just walking by and he hit you?" my friend asks.

"Maybe I looked at him the wrong way," I say.

"I don't know what I'd do if that happened to me,"

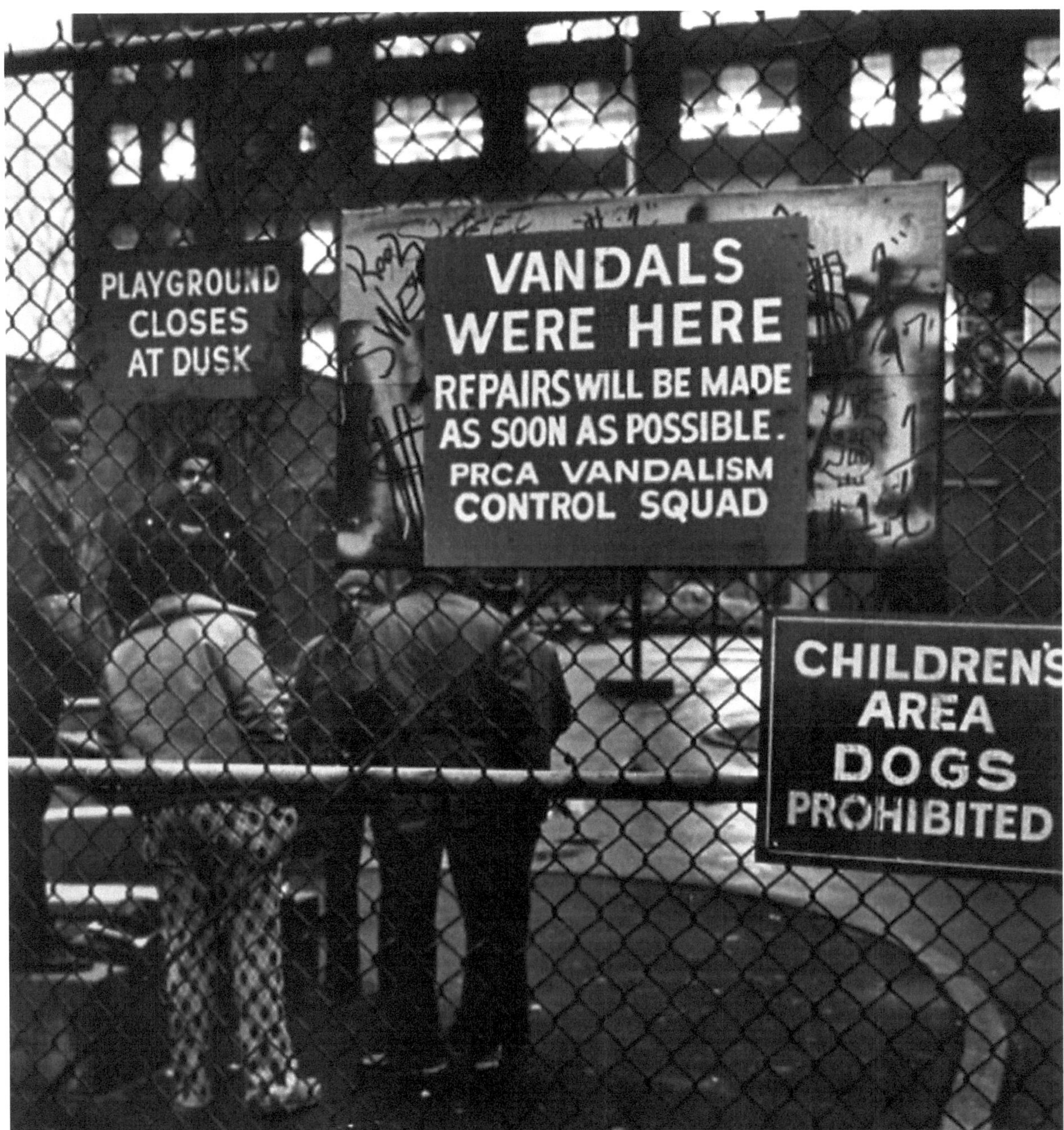

Photograph by Charles Gatewood

my friend says.

My friend is a big guy, and I wonder if he means he would hit back.

"I might do something," he adds as he makes a fist on the table.

Near the end of the meal, an older woman who is sitting near us comes over. She knows my friend—they are both members of the club—but she wants to talk to me. "Let me see your left hand," she said. "Are you wearing a wedding ring?"

"Why?" I asked.

"I want to find someone for my daughter," she said. "I'm looking for a man of about 50."

Maybe I look like I fit the part. It doesn't matter, though; I don't want to be matched up with anyone.

"She's right here," the woman says.

Sure enough, there is a young woman at a nearby table. She is standing to leave. Her mother motions her over, and the daughter shakes my hand and says hello.

"She's a lawyer," her mother says, "but she doesn't practice. She works pro bono."

The daughter is attractive, younger than 50. Any bachelor in the club would be a good candidate for her.

Unfortunately, I'm wearing a ring, and I show it to the mother. After that, I know I'm not going to get a business card or a phone number for her daughter.

*

I take the subway to get home. On my way, I don't see the usual musician on the platform. The older man who plays a wooden flute and makes notes that sound like wind through trees isn't there. Instead, I see a man who has a poetry display. He has a cardboard table with papers on it and sign that says, "Published Poet, New York Times." Another sign is propped on the concrete floor. It says: "Watch TheLivingPoet on Youtube.com." The small text says he'll write poems on demand, for a fee.

When I walk toward him, he says, "I'm the poet."

I ask if he'll write a poem about violence.

He says he won't. "I'm a poet of peace," he says.

I offer to pay him.

"You should pay for peace, not violence," he says. "Where are you from, anyway?"

"I'm from Pennsylvania, but my mother is Chinese," I say. "She was a Chinese person living in China; she wasn't an American in China."

"What the hell are you talking about?" the poet says.

"Some people don't understand," I say, "so I have to clarify."

*

Later, I tell my wife about the potential match-up.

"Do you think they were playing with you?" she asks.

"No," I say. "I think they were serious. I could have called one of them, the mother or the daughter. I could have made a date."

"You're going to give me bad dreams," my wife says.

*

The next day, when I go to the subway, I look for the published poet, but he is gone. The stairs where he lives and writes are swept clear. Apparently, it is not permitted to live and write poetry in the subway.

The next day, when I go to the subway, I look for the published poet, but he is gone. The stairs where he lives and writes are swept clear. Apparently, it is not permitted to live and write poetry in the subway.

I wonder if he's gone deeper into the tunnel network. There's an unused station halfway to the next stop—I've seen it when I ride. No trains stop there, but some dim lights illuminate the platform. The walls are covered with graffiti. It might be a good place for a poet who doesn't want to be disturbed.

I look down the track from where I'm standing, and I think I see the glow of that ghost station. The published poet might be living there.

Contours of the Irreal: Paintings by David de Biasio

Erik Noonan

ALTHOUGH IT MAY STRIKE A THEORIST AS paradoxical, the artist's sole response to a moment such as ours—with its ideological cowardice, its reflexive violence, its prurient spectatorship—is always to exult in using the most voluptuous and rigorous resources at hand, to offer the public something that will be the equal of our condition, with unbounded patience and tenderness, in the service of an open luxuriance of the imagination, a lavish strictness, an arduous delight, which everyone shares, no matter how fully or for how long the sensate mind we all have in common

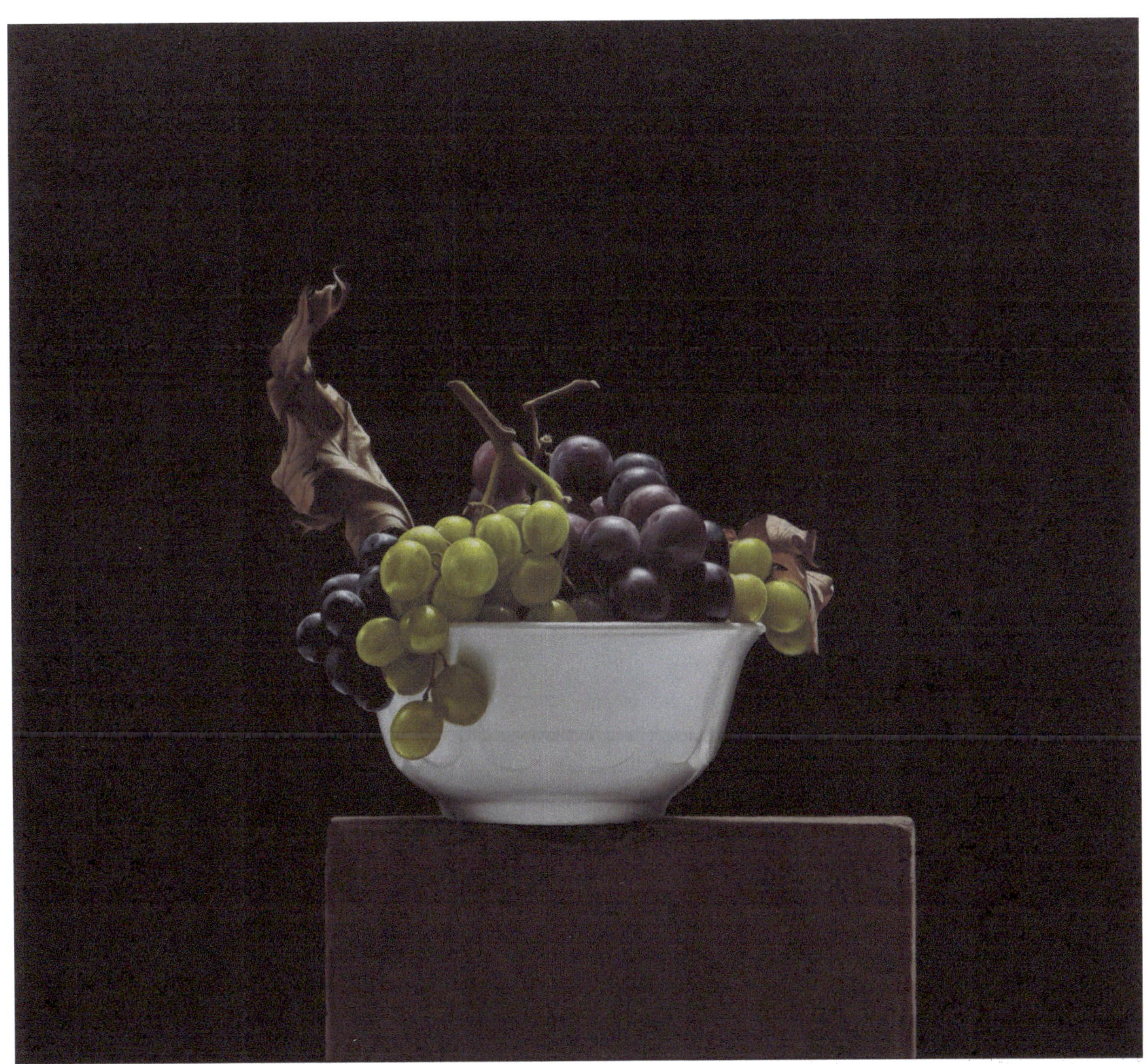

Vortical Being, 2008, oil on linen, 66 x 58 cm

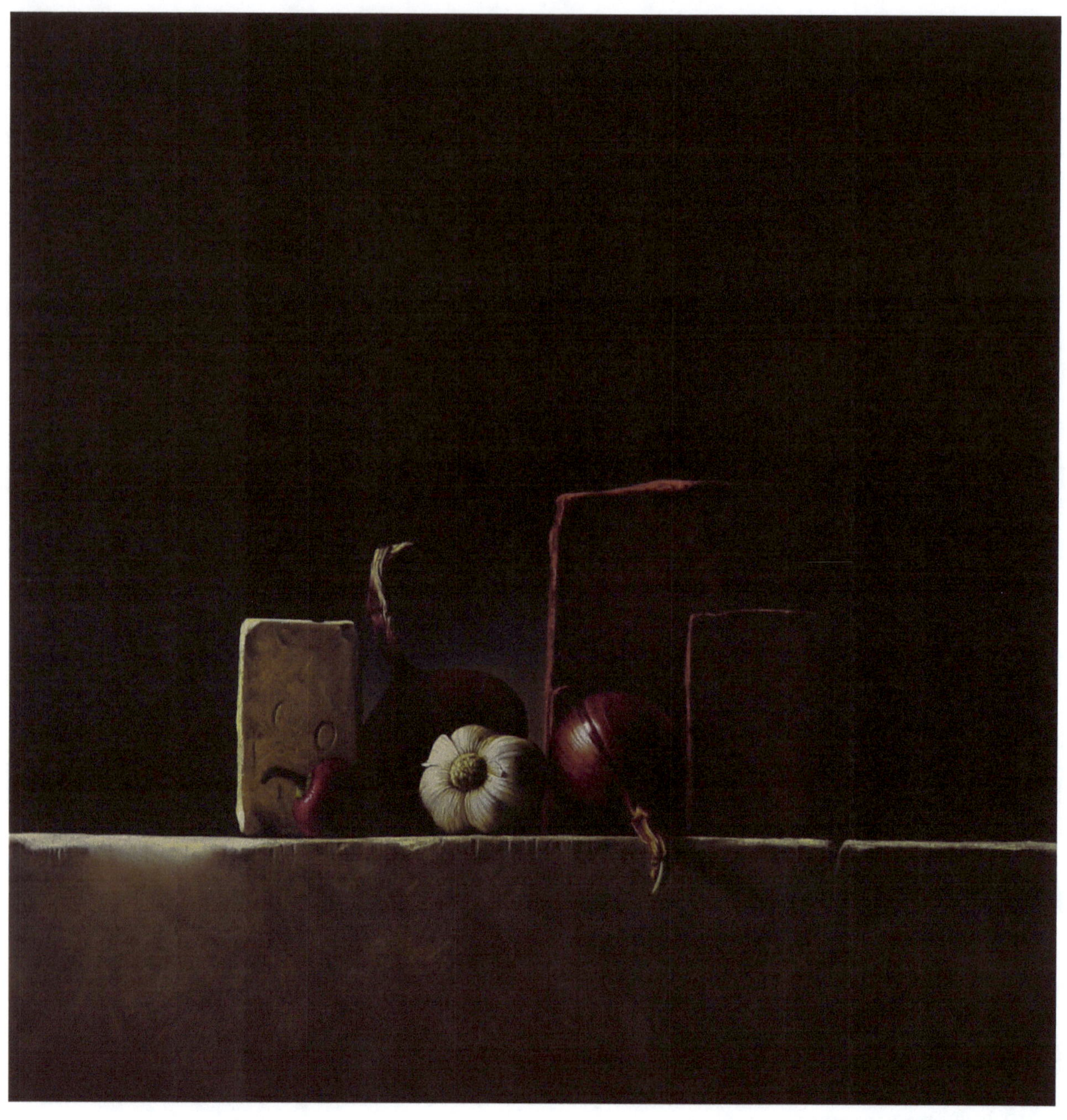

#7, 2006, oil on linen, 60 x 60 cm

might be suppressed or forgotten. In the paintings of David de Biasio, we encounter a general circumstance as it appears in the reflection of an exquisitely refined sensibility, as if the mental eye were cleansed of expectancy and reminiscence, and we saw through disappointment and joy like so much glass, to the things beyond them: these artworks induce an alternate, creative condition in viewers by which we, along with the artist, realize the inapprehensible in images, suspending belief and disbelief.

With their subtly pure yet pervasive and obstinate artistry, de Biasio's paintings recall the offhand charm of Chardin or the clinical ardor of Cotán. In this respect it makes sense when we read that Alberto

Agazzani feels de Biasio's style is "so totally arrogant in its perfection and in the stupefying play of light, shadows, and reflections, that it defies any attempt at a reading in any way hyperrealist." If Agazzani means by this that he thinks the perfection and light-play in these paintings are arrogant because they stubbornly retain or reinsert a note of individual interpretation or perception into the sacrosanct canons of the hyperrealist movement, then I agree and, in fact, instead of obsolete designations, I offer the term *irreal* to describe the work of David de Biasio and other young artists who are now working more or less in concert with his efforts in this direction.

The advance of these new Irreal Painters upon hyperrealism—against which their work reacts and from which it grew—may be seen in their successful attempts to restore objecthood to the position of the theme of a painting, by expunging all traces of anecdote from the work. Along with this tendency, these painters have recognized that for the viewer, simplicity only emerges from a canvas through the mediation of the utmost technical sophistication; and this is why, in their studios, so much manipulation of things and images has taken place before any pigment is applied to a canvas.

While de Biasio's more traditional still lifes observe the genre's conventions, we would be mistaken to infer from this the espousal of an achieved prosperity, tranquil and secure, *à la* the Netherlandish Golden Age. You have to ask how the pictures engage your private stock of skills and memories and habits; who needs what they've already got? We're not memory banks to be crammed with information: the painting knows the eye, knows the way we see. A common and telling sight in produce markets, for example, is the stranger who regards a food item with the sense that it provides a unique sort of data about the society in which it is sown, grown, harvested, processed, distributed, sold, purchased, prepared, cooked and consumed. Looking at fruit and vegetables is a way of *dishing on* society, if you'll pardon the expression. This gossipy, almost tabloidesque glimpse into an intimate domain reveals what is and isn't the case, in a way that no other inquiry can; and when such an insight reaches us by way of a fictive gaze that's been put forward by a still life painter, its exposures are doubly revealing—and this is multiplied many times over yet again when the painter is Italian, his country troubled by the third year of a recession, with total unemployment at twelve-point-six percent and youth unemployment at forty-two percent, and with anti-austerity protests surging into clashes against the police. In such a state of affairs, a picture of foodstuffs that aren't staples embodies an articulate silence indeed, both palpable and ethereal in its gorgeousness. And the choice of items ramifies further as well: most of these edibles can't be kept in cold storage for long, they are native to the region,

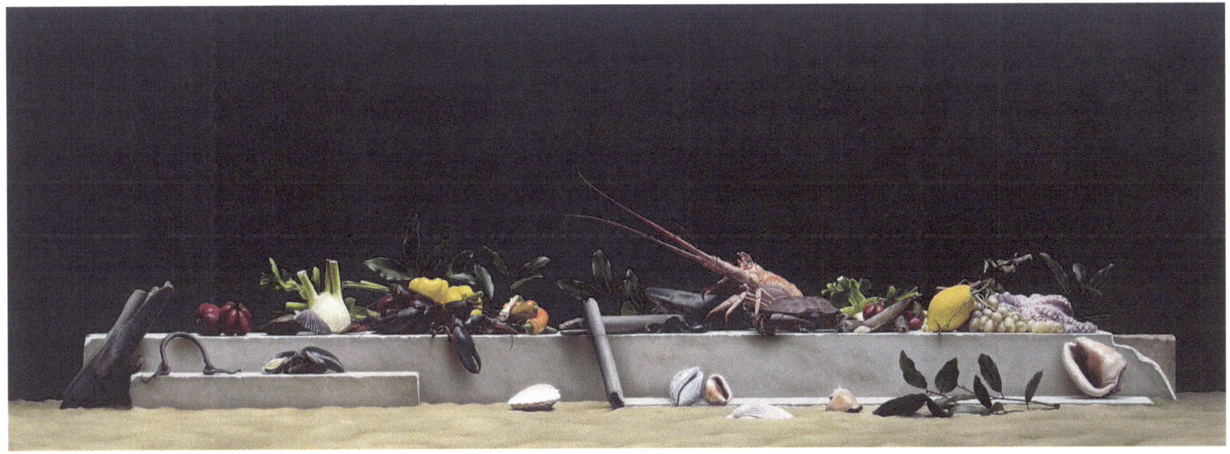

Marea, 2009, oil on linen, 300 x 100 cm

they're instinct with Mediterranean civilization and culture, they're ancient and new.

These things (peppers, tomatoes, onions, persimmons, grapes, lemons, plums, cherries, pears, blueberries, apples, pomegranates, lobsters, crabs, octopi, twigs, leaves, driftwood, marble, stones, shells, sand, wax paper) are objects that stand in distinct if difficult relation with their subjects (us)—taken into the sensorium via perspectives and sizes which propose a scaled grandeur, situated as far from monumentality as it is from miniaturism, eschewing both sublimity and quaintness. The camera angles and stretcher dimensions take their place in a procedure that amounts to a series of safeguards against the all-too-human instinct for hyperbole. Technical details direct the artist's energies—of which there are vast reserves—and moderation, judiciousness and tact indicate a temperament that's not overeager to dispense with the complexity of its expression, or to stand exposed as anything but a single worker among many in a shop where images are made.

The presence and the character of light in these paintings can't be overemphasized. The earliest available digital still life images (the untitled canvas #7 for instance) admit a dim and severe Caravaggesque luminosity, from a source located somewhere outside the picture plane, moving into an enclosed and oppressive pictorial space, a confined gloom, that has the somber effect of pushing objects up close and into a shallow foreground, uneasily; while in several

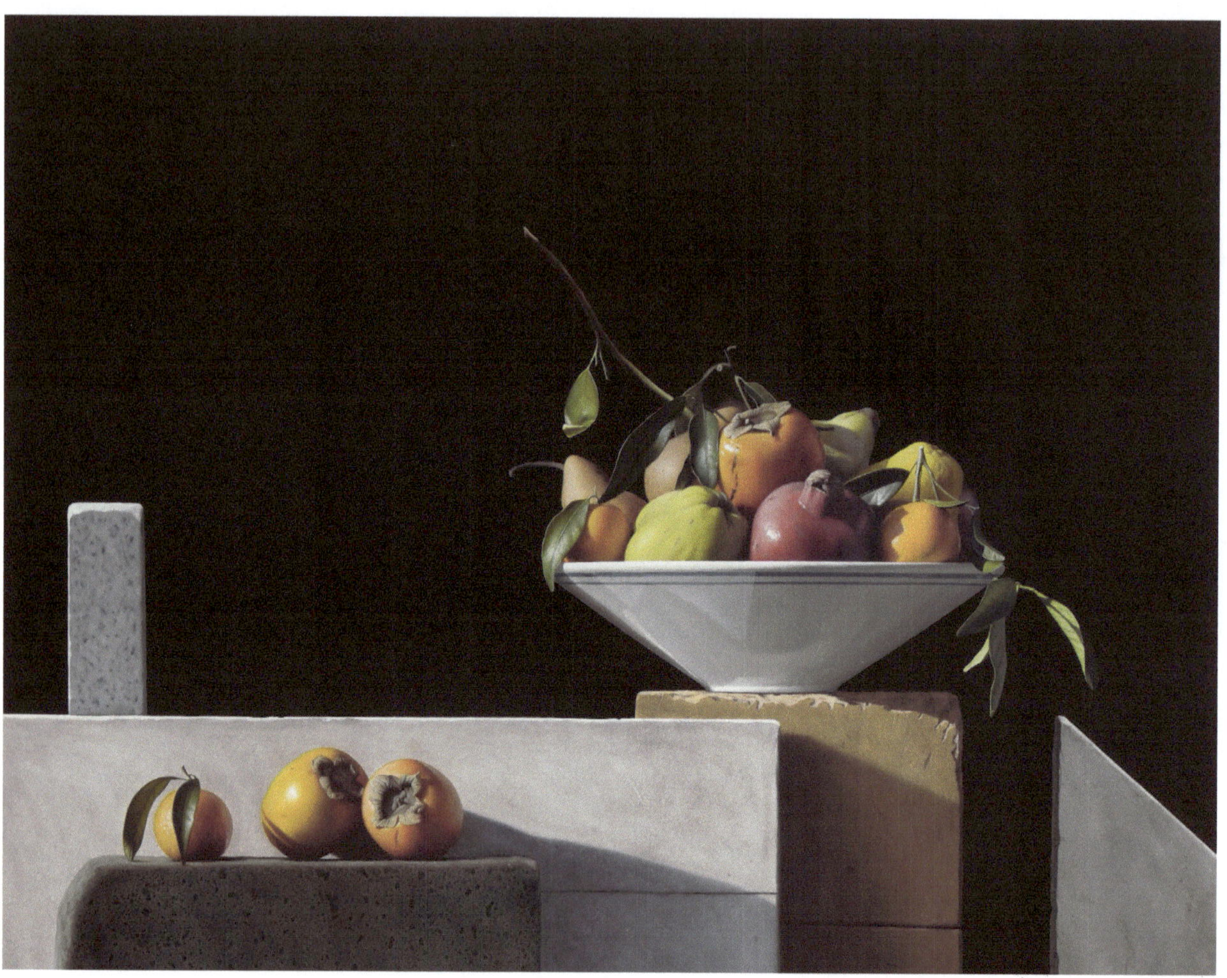

Autumnal Offering, 2009, oil on linen, 120 x 100 cm

later pictures (such as *Vortical Being*), a cool diffuse gleam descends evenly throughout and scatters its justice impartially over all, enfolding fruit and ware and marble in an effulgence that bespeaks an equable directing of the attention outward toward both organic life and the works of humankind: it's a light in which ordinary objects seem again to possess acuity, its dignified vibrancy, its easy way with commerce, its gentleness of cast shadow, its valediction to—and critique of—the (hyper)real, its intimation of decay and death.

Even aside from de Biasio's technical virtuosity, the anterior facts that underpin any given picture are so far from anything we can construe as per-

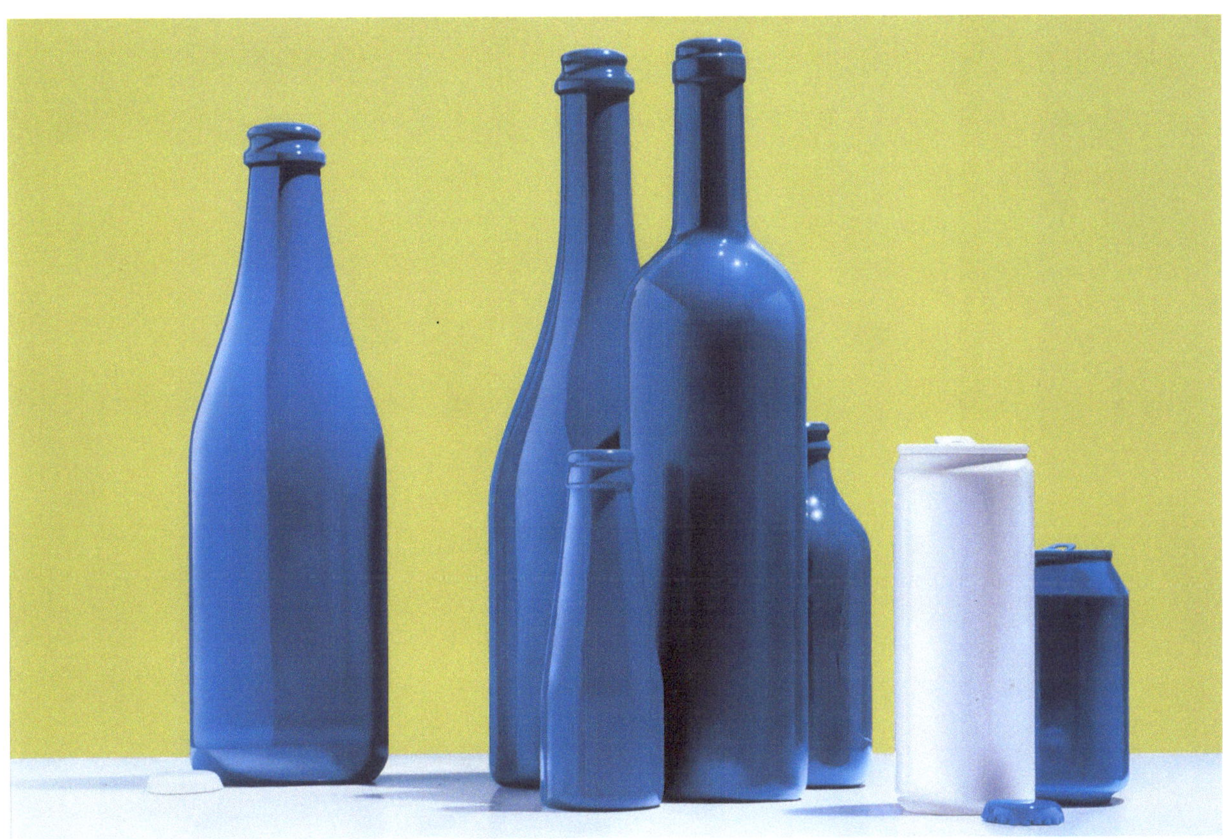

No Logo #91, 2011, oil on linen, 60 x 60 cm

luminescence, as they were once thought to—marine, Northern, and tolerant. This quality reaches its most eloquent and sensuous elaboration in the astonishing *Marea,* before maturing into a kind of souvenir of infinity in *Autumnal Offering* with the warm declining glow of a melancholy resignation and a bountiful harvest. Altogether these several types of light unite with a newfound color sense (de Biasio notably cites Raphael and Titian among his inspirations), and a surety and concision in *Still Life #116,* absolutely de Biasio's masterpiece to date, a magnificent statement, with its piquant dailiness, its seeming naturalness, its sonal that we're forced to recognize the paintings' oblique relationship not only to nature but to identity as well. This is a painter who practices still life as the production of a likeness not of things but of the conversation between psyche and intellect, a representation that doesn't avoid unflattering tones, or strike flattering ones. In the same way that our optical equipment supplies bulk and heft to the space between two emphatically drawn lines, and complements an insistent red with a green of its own, so too does the preconscious mind provide the subject-object transformation of a thing on a canvas with

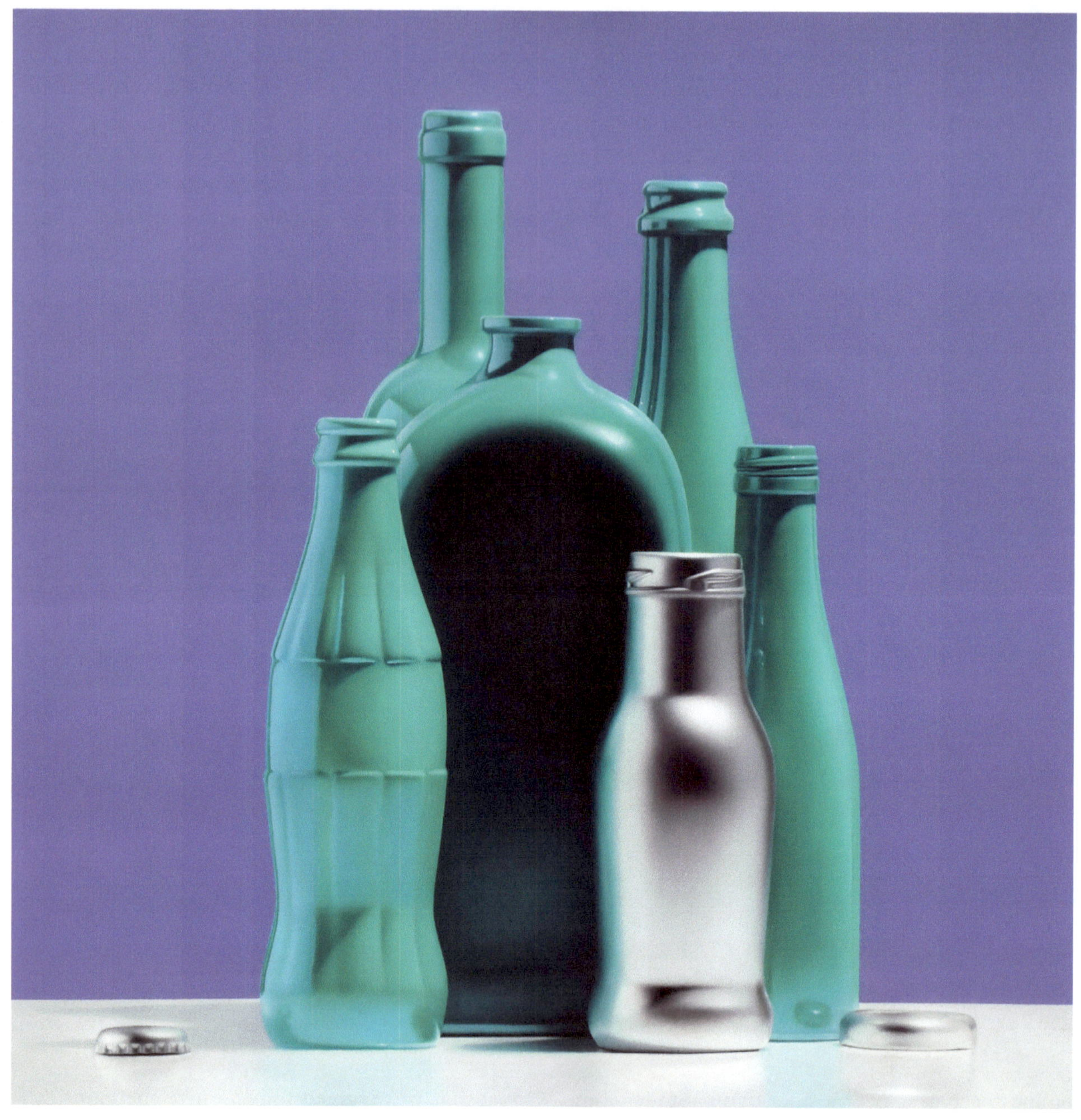

No Logo #100, 2011, oil on linen, 100 x 100 cm

thematic coordinates that are commensurate with the emotional tones it finds there. This is totally different from painting that "tells a story." As a student at the Fine Arts Academy of Rome, de Biasio wrote his thesis on Gustave Moreau, a copy of which is now housed in the Gustave Moreau Museum in Paris. De Biasio remarks: "Obviously in my recent work it is very difficult to detect my interest in Moreau but he was surely one of the artists who contributed the most to my growing passion for art." For Moreau, a painter of mythological and Biblical scenes, the context was a crisis of religion, as the new rationalist doctrines of his day attacked established articles of faith; his theme was a desire that had not been corrupted into lust. In light of Moreau's impact upon this artist, we may conjecture that the overarching context of De

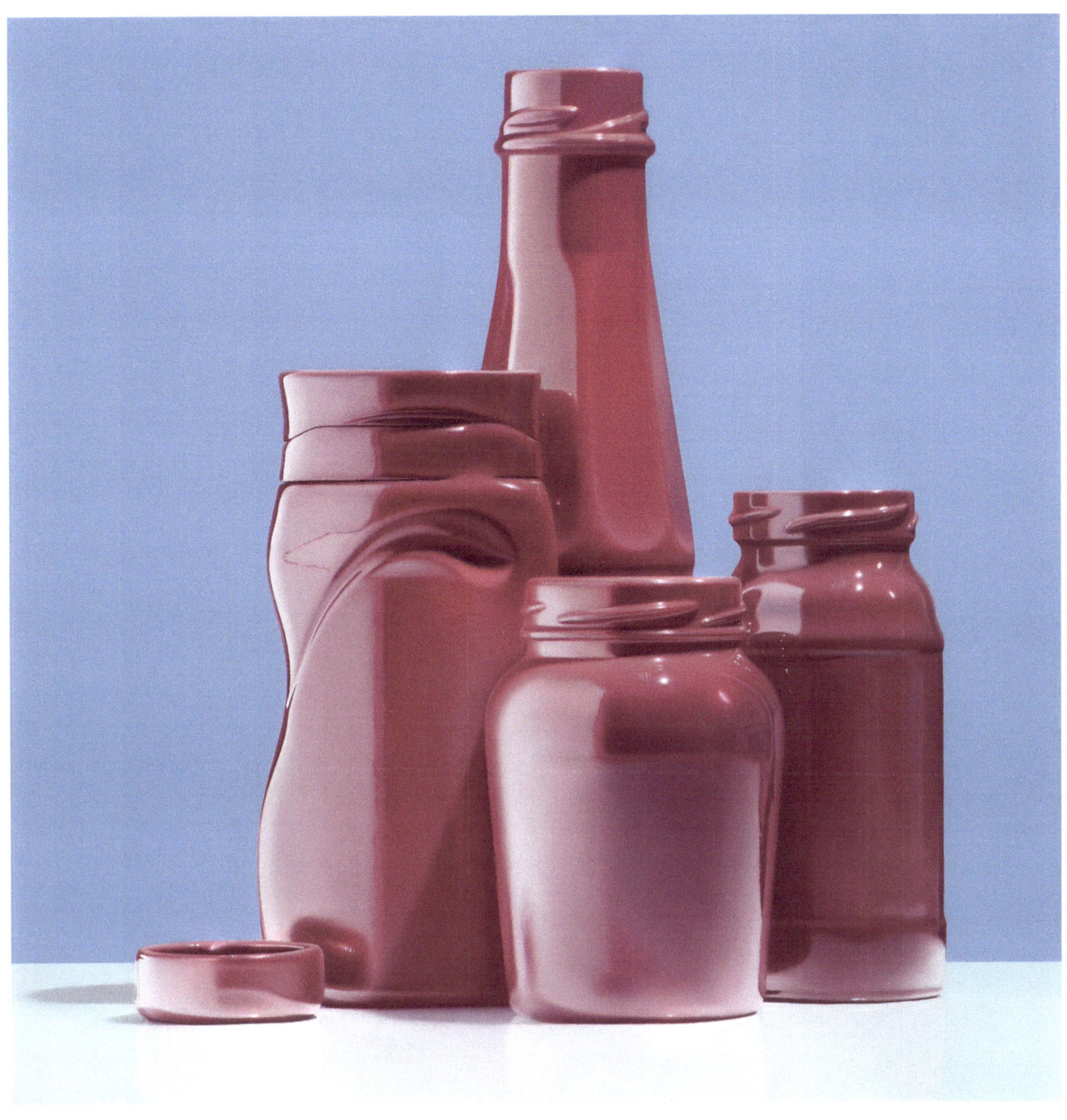

No Logo #92, 2011, oil on linen, 60 x 60 cm

Biasio's art is the silhouette of bourgeois behavior as it mutates under globalization, and that his theme is a desire that hasn't been commodified. True, the combined effects of mechanized industry and centralized secular authority have produced the new conformism that's obvious to everyone, but the disturbing presence of such sameness in the visual domain of our lives, in the most quotidian of things, isn't easy to perceive, let alone envision. De Biasio depicts this presence—or rather, this absence—with a traditionalism and a reticence that evade the ready replies of those who remain spiritual casualties, those who *are* the theme and who therefore can't pick up on it, or still others again, who dismiss the systemic dread of these days as deluded or childish, and instead eulogize consumer experience with references to prestige food, prestige clothing, prestige art, and so on.

Delightfully, with the elaboration of the *No Logo*

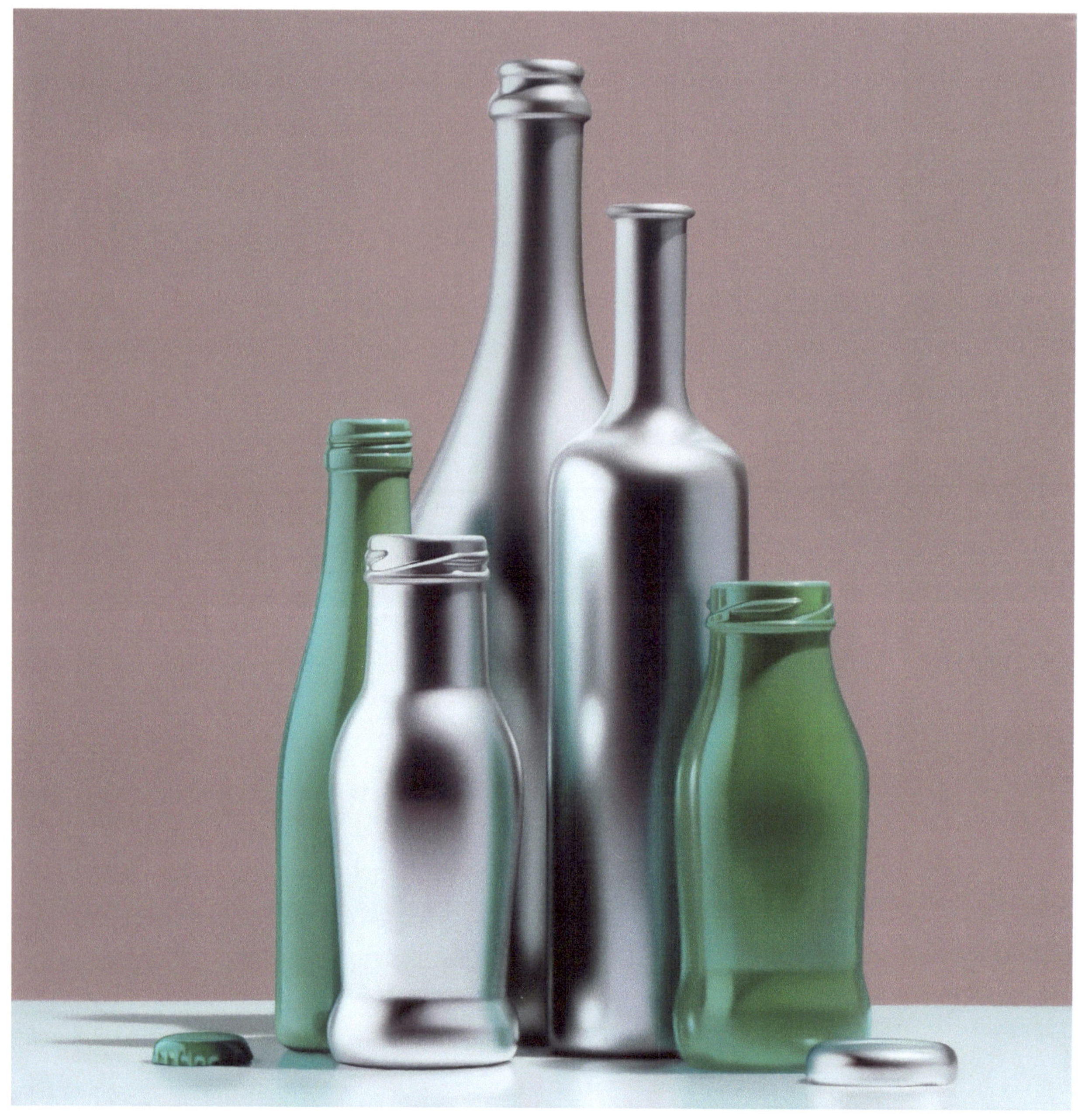

No Logo #93, 2011, oil on linen, 60 x 60 cm

series, the implications of de Biasio's thesis on Gustave Moreau begin to find an articulation that would be hard to ignore even if it weren't so thoroughly enchanting: the self-conscious academic paganism of Moreau's illustrations from the Greco-Judaeo-Christian mythological corpus lent a fragile embodiment to the intense collective nostalgia of a wildly insecure moment. His figures are already throwbacks—way back. Biasio's paintings are really not still lifes at all of course, but moments, scenes in our own mythological narrative. It is both cruel and generous that the nostalgia and mythology, even the narrative, all only seem to have been excised, made conspicuous by their absence.

Of this next series following the still lifes, de Biasio writes: "As you may know, *No Logo* is an essay written by the Canadian journalist Naomi Klein. The book is about branding and the no-global movement, of which *No Logo* is considered one of the main reference texts. I decided to place my project *No Logo* against this background." Klein's thesis in *No Logo* (1999) is that the drastically increased wealth, political influence, and cultural sway of multinational corporations, which for better or worse we thinking up ideas,' said New York artist and former [Jeff] Koons studio assistant Jaclyn Santos. 'To [Koons], it's not about making a work physically, it's about making the idea.'" By divorcing himself from the physical workmanship of art, the artist-as-businessman-as-iconoclast, ultramodern and slick,

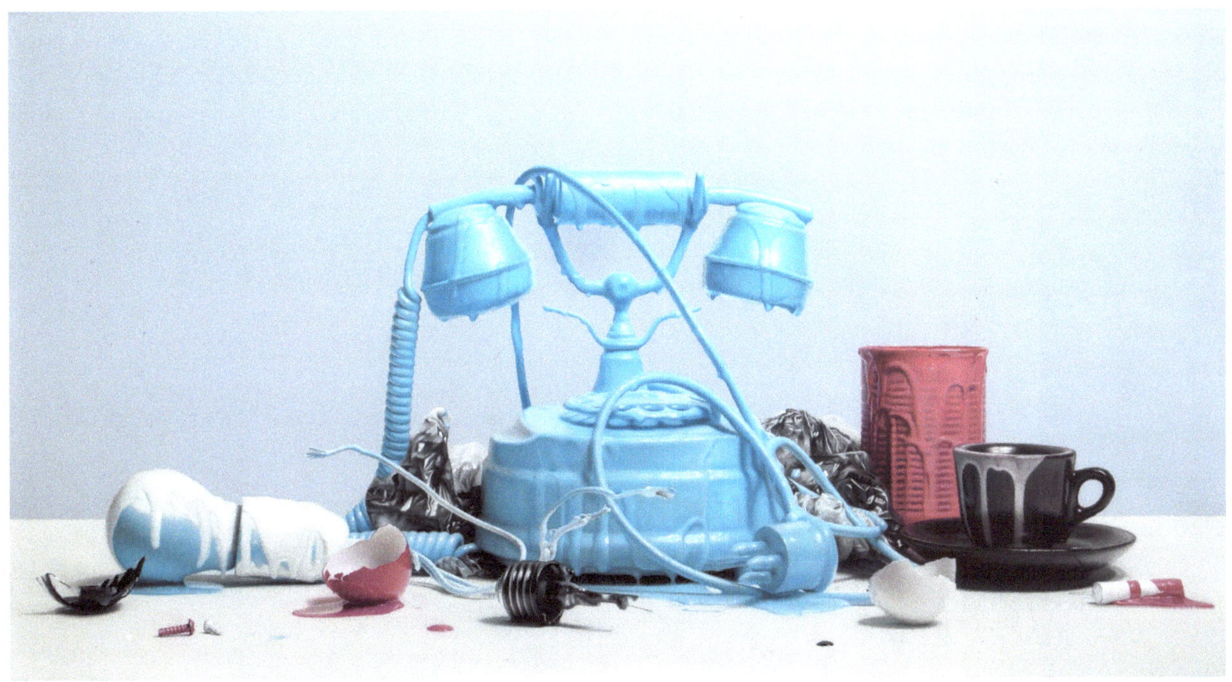

Dripping Memory #114, 2013, oil on linen, 150 x 80 cm

now recognize as normal, have come to pass according to the pronouncements of certain economists and marketing professionals, who predicted back in the mid-1980s how the success of any company on a worldwide scale would depend upon its ability to produce not only material goods but also a brand which could conceptualize its products for a mass consumer audience according to standardized socioeconomic status signifiers. The facts have borne Klein out, and then some. To see that this occurrence has had tremendous consequences for artists and art lovers, we may turn to no less distinguished an art periodical than the *Wall Street Journal:* "'People have a concept of how an artist works—they imagine Jackson Pollock pouring paint over a canvas, they definitely don't imagine a man in an office in a suit beats out the primitivist, obsolete, semi-articulate bohemian, with his baby paint set (but no easel), in a zero-sum spectator-sport battle over the spoils of twenty-first century capital: a global art world for the neoconservative millennium, made up of inseparable binary pairs ruthlessly pitted against each other by a sublime and malignant Nature. And the victor, a recipient of the U.S. State Department Medal of Arts—able to bypass the traditional material procedures of art by outsourcing them to his staff while blithely traipsing along en route to material wealth—delivers a foolproof prescription for success in this arena; it turns out that the rest of us could all win, too, exactly like him, if only we'd just *relax*. From *The New Yorker:* "I believe that my journey has really been to remove my own anxiety.

That's the key. The more anxiety you can remove, the more free you are to make that gesture, whatever the gesture is. The dialogue is first with the artist, but then it goes outward, and is shared with other people. And if the anxiety is removed everything is so close, everything is available, and it's just this little bit of confidence, or trust, that people have to delve into." In Naomi Klein's words, this anxiety-free gestural liberation of commercial art (USD $54 million for *Balloon Dog [Orange]* at Christie's in 2013) sports the guise of—that's right—"the impenetrable abyss gaping underneath the Big Bubble and engulfing its love in darkness when it bursts and every last dime rains down just like real money.

It comes as no surprise to learn that de Biasio's extended period of residence and study in New York, while working as an assistant to painter Mark Kostabi, helped give rise to the *No Logo* paintings: "I have to say that the Kostabi job was fantastic," he recalls. "It allowed me to live deep in the New York artistic atmosphere and become familiar with a way of working which is totally different from the one I

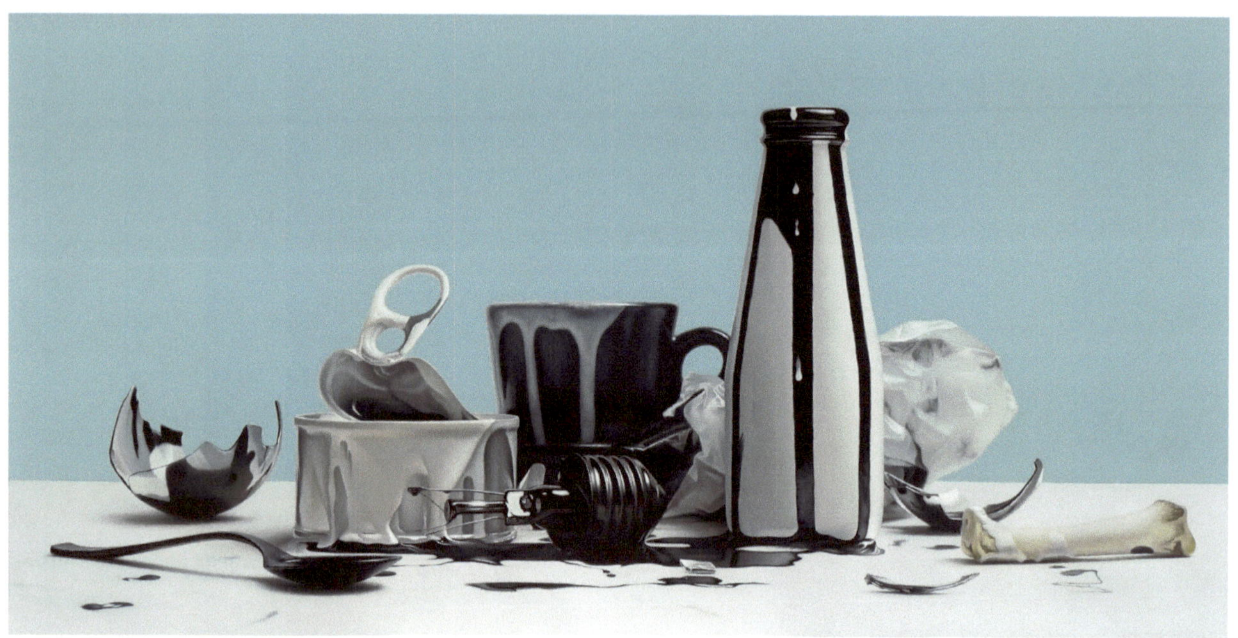

Dripping Memory #115, 2014, oil on linen, 100 x 60 cm

shiny surfaces of branded culture." The mask has long since fused with the face that wears it. The high media profile of megatrend amalgam art inflates the Multiple and the Readymade of yore into an absurd caricature, fetishized repro tech where all emotions are constants in a logical system, and bathos rules in a particolored leisure park where fun is coextensive with one's ability not to get sidetracked by bothersome reflections, questions, doubts, misgivings—in short, by any impulse which might give rise to nuance: because that's the one thing which would turn the pocket void of this spastic milieu into an knew in Italy. Moreover I got to know a lot of artists. The New York experience left a tangible sign in my subsequent work, particularly in the chromatic evolution." We see this development in *No Logo #91.* If such color choices indicate an American palette (he has mentioned Thiebaud as an influence), then the character of the composition as a whole is markedly Italian: "I give a lot of importance to the compositional technique of my still lifes," de Biasio continues. "Every single object has to be positioned in the right place. There must be a sort of 'dialogue' (chromatic and volumetric) between the elements, and here there is the significance of Morandi's lesson." The small, almost shimmering tableaux of tightly grouped vessels in muted pinks, creams, yellows and greens, painstakingly rendered by the assiduous and withdrawn master Giorgio Morandi—who painted them as if in an act of prayer, and who famously claimed that there is nothing more surreal than the real itself—might seem to be a far cry from the high polish of the *No Logo* series, but the effect of Morandi on de Biasio's process can be discerned in his paintings' utter lack of cleverness, in their unironic, declarative fontality, as in *No Logo #92, #93* and *#100.*

The artist recognizes not only that he can't help expressing his own time, but also that he does so tangentially as it were, hardly beside the point or from outside, but rather complementary to his age, apposite. In the case of this painter particularly, we witness a supreme intuition into the evolving character of twenty-first century cognitive style: here are paintings that don't just acknowledge the end of chemical photography, and the advent of the painter's studio as a Dark Room where all manner of implements establish the conditions under which at last the artist may track and study the behavior of paint instead of the conventions of representation: much more, de Biasio presents us with these works of his as one who is exceptionally aware of the craft of painting, yes, but also of its advantageous position *vis-à-vis* his society and its culture. He has contributed a piece to that odd genre, the Artist Video—but as you might expect, he completely ignores its potential as a marketing tool and opts to use only muzak for the soundtrack and to depict not his face but only his hand as it puts paint on linen with a fan brush: a gentle but firm counterstatement. When we watch this clip on the screen of a device, its imagery welcomes us into a painter's studio, where we imagine that the disembodied hand we see applying paint to a canvas is really our own; in the same way, when we view one of the *No Logo* paintings exhibited on a gallery wall, the rich and subtle real paint immerses

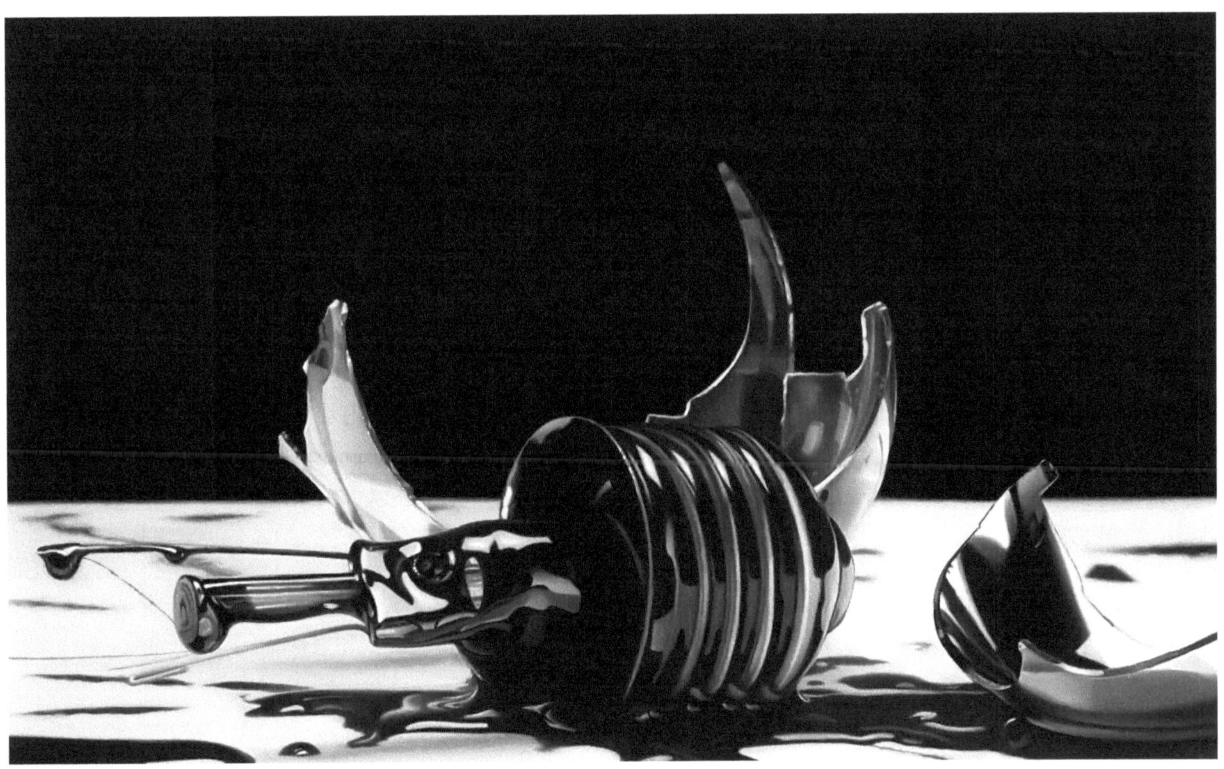

Dripping Memory #118, 2014, oil on linen, 100 x 60 cm

our minds in a solution of dark energy, where we dissolve into the aether and breathe a spirit that infuses the cosmos with force and motion, so that we see the way light dwells, and bind the sweet influences of the Pleiades, and loose the bands of Orion.

The viewer, the subject, looks at the paintings, the things in the paintings are objects in the viewer's life but they aren't the object of the painting, the object of the painting is the paint, if not then one remains merely a viewer and never becomes the subject. It's a contract, both sides have to try. The painter whose awareness of these conditions is acute runs the risk of being too self-conscious about it, overdoing the modeling of paint and losing the viewer's attention. De Biasio's allusion to "a certain expressive tension" in his recent works indicates a tension not among the things depicted but between the distinct reality of the pigment and a performance of illusionism, it's a tension that makes our perception flicker between paint and painted. He creates a representation of the pictorial representation of optical facts, a sophisticated performance, for sure.

The encoded figural themes known in the visual arts as *Pathosformel* or feeling-forms have gathered together into conventions over centuries, but they only emerge in an artwork in spite of the Will, as philosophy defines it. It's not that pretense to knowledge of every possible context would offend modesty (because some artists are overconfident) but rather that, if one does not "lose oneself" in making the artwork, the seed of narrative that one's content contains will not have a chance to grow, shed its casing and become a theme. Still Life is called *Nature Morte* for a reason. As a genre it automatically gives rise to a theme known in the sciences as the Observer Effect, in philosophy as *das Ding an Sich* or "the thing in itself" (Kant and Nietzsche) and as the *phenomenon* and *noumenon,* or Form and Idea, of Plato.

De Biasio's latest project, the nascent *Dripping Memory* series, bears the mark of an analytical poetics, directing an indulgent but exacting gaze toward the tropes of canonical post-surrealist dream logic in its passé approach to rendering unconscious processes. "In *Dripping Memory,* objects are immersed in a varnish that forms a patina," the painter tells us. "This covers the object, modifying the outline, as if the memory of that same object were disappearing." (See *Dripping Memory #114, #115,* and *#118.*) We may be forgiven for surmising that a corollary of this most recent series abides in the lengthy agglutinating of cathexes by the libido and their subsequent identification in psychotherapy. An icy, almost colorless zone opens before us in these pictures, strewn with obsolete gadgetry, disused furnishings and broken hardware, all covered in goo of various hues that appears to have dried and hardened over each piece of junk into a gleaming shell even as it oozes down onto the surface underneath. The *Dripping Memory* paintings are the very picture of a Freudian *Unheimliche,* "the uncanny," in their imaging of what you might call the psychic viscosity of things.

At a minimum it is reasonable to surmise that despite the trendspotting ambitions that prevail in right-thinking critical and social media circles of art theory opinion ("highbrow taste, mass appeal," to be sure), an apparent lack of emphasis in an oil painter's treatment of his motifs—which moreover he has chosen for their affect, as emotive stimuli—far from testifying to a crisis in painting, proves its health beyond cavil finally by asserting that the integrity of human life dwells within a kind of nonheroic ambience, a potent aura of thought. It's not just that pigment isn't a consequence of things any more than words are, but also that once this fact has been grasped, the artist has to synthesize a plurality of extrinsic elements he only now sees in their interrelations, as if for the first time, each one by itself and every one together. If there is any vehemence to be found in the art of David de Biasio, surely it resides within this aesthetic and in his fixity there.

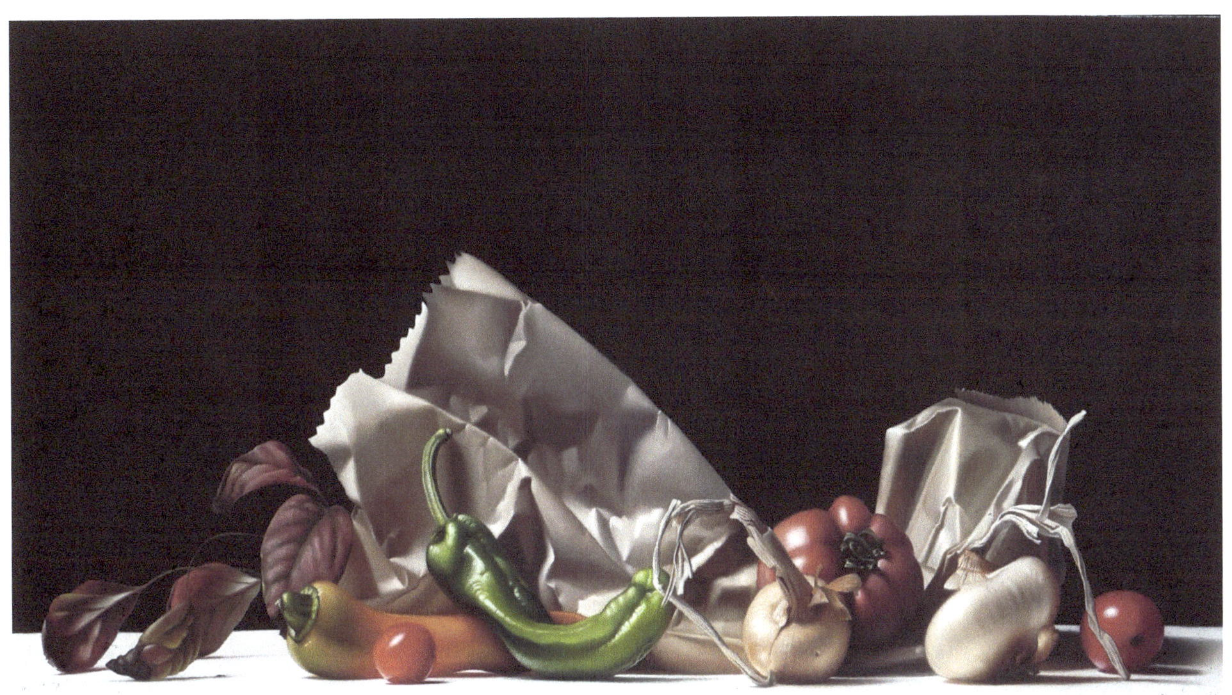

Still Life #116, 2014, oil on linen, 100 x 60 cm

This article quotes from: Alberto Agazzani, "No Logo," *Cose mentali, a cura di Alberto Agazzani,* Gagliardi Edizioni, 2011.

The author gratefully acknowledges the generous assistance of David de Biasio, as well as that of Lauren J. Ellis, Director of CK Contemporary, San Francisco, California.

Welcome to All the Pleasures

Robert C. Hardin

My father liked to say that I'd always been impossible to find. During birth, he recalled, I couldn't be extracted with forceps. No one could see me, so I made my own way out of my mother. The midwife only located me after following my cries and throwing a towel over the delivery table. Rubber gloves prodded me and a blanket swaddled me; naked hands passed through me.

Which is why, in my only memory of her, my mother failed to catch me in her bare arms and shouted my name as I fell and flattened against the kitchen linoleum. She kept calling for me while her Abyssinian cat skidded off. Moments later, it returned.

It wanted to verify my presence but couldn't even graze my torso. I reached up from the floor to stroke its fur—fingers thrumming the buttons of the trumpet valves of the air—and missed, as I did so often in the early years. The cat proved as impalpable to me as the other mammals I encountered. Dogs never met my spectral grip, nor could I menace the occasional rat. Insects were the only form of life that I could touch. That ever found a way to touch me in return.

The earliest faces I can recall stared past me with expressions of panic. The provenance of my shrieks eluded them. All loomed hugely until only one face remained: Father's face, as he dropped a blanket over the floor to reveal my shape.

"Now I'll always be able to find you," he said.

For sixteen years, I lived in an enclosure in his basement. As I continued to grow, he fitted me with a succession of muzzles and masks. They made my whereabouts obvious and my vulnerability reliable.

He wanted me to understand him, so he taught me how to read with old newspapers and secondhand textbooks. After a while, we switched to encyclopedia volumes. I remember being forced to learn the List of Physical Constants and feeling an apple peeler slice my arm whenever I made a mistake. Eventually, I could recite the sequence in a monotone.

One night, he drank too much and stumbled down the basement steps looking for amusement. He staggered over to the litter box, grabbed a handful of cat shit and flung it at me. "Better to see you with," he slurred. He tried to jab me with a rake handle, steadying himself by holding onto the mesh at the top of my enclosure. After a few minutes of one-sided swordplay, he slid against the bars between us and passed out.

I took that opportunity to steal his keys and smash in his skull.

My escape was so easy that after I'd cleared the area, I doubled back to stand at the threshold of Father's house. I crossed my arms in defiance: no one could have guessed what I did. Anyone who'd ever known about me or witnessed my gifts was gone.

Truthfully, I felt as naïve about them as they had to be about me. How they lived, how their cars worked—everything was new. I hung around for a week watching strangers ring the doorbell. After they went back in their houses, I taught myself to drive by wrecking their SUVs.

I decided to leave town after noticing all the bus stops. I couldn't drive very well and mass transit was a blast. I stood in the aisles as if I owned them and the bus drivers were my chauffeurs. I set off alarms out of inexperience, then boredom, pushing through turnstiles and gates. I sauntered through train cars tearing trivial objects from desperate people's hands.

I found I couldn't sleep in public places. Trying to rest among adults was wrenching and children were terrifying. I never got used to the claw hands that boys made when they sensed I was there, fingers contracting and snatching at the source of their

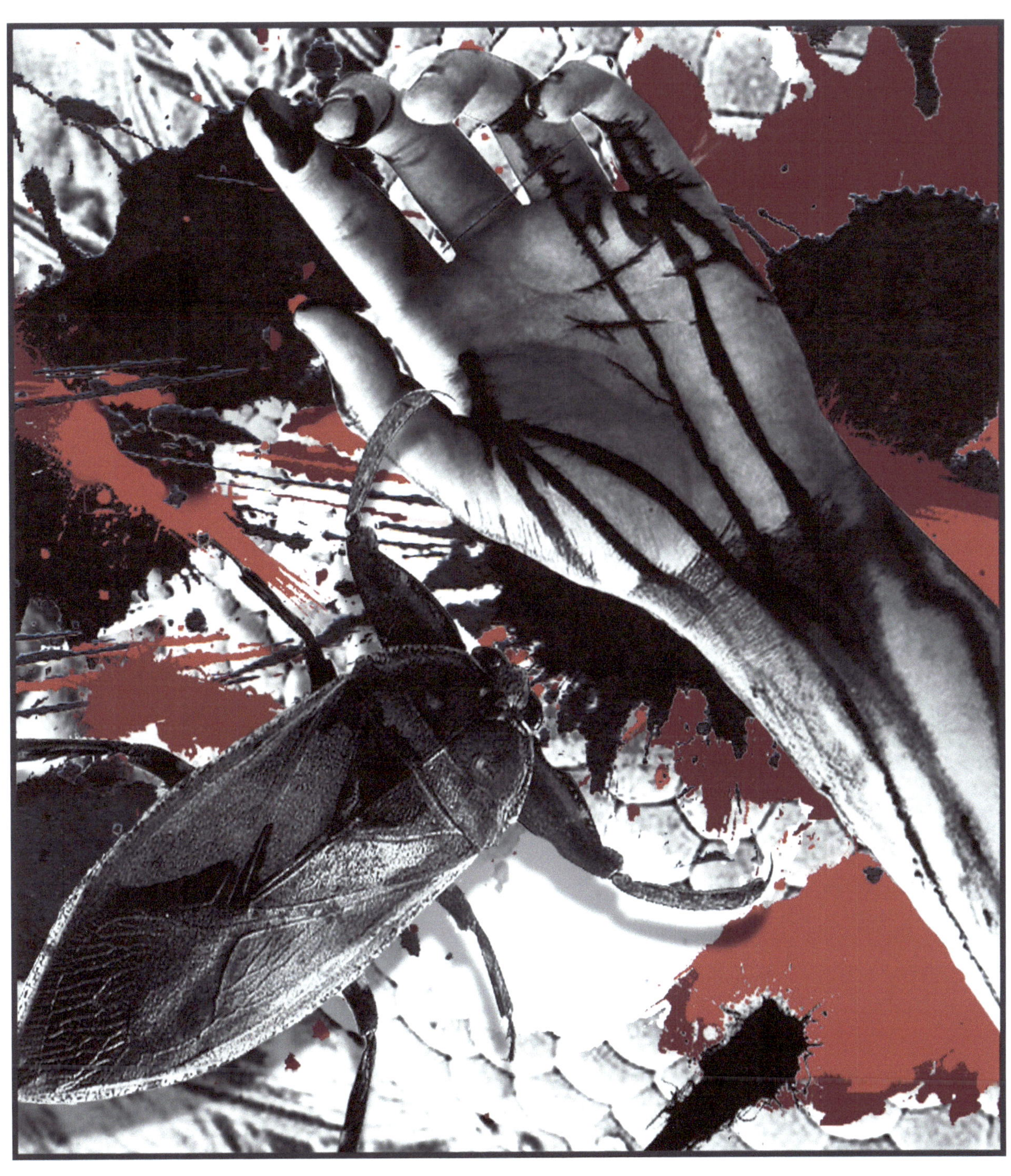

Bitten, mixed media by Leslie Hardie

displeasure.

Unrented apartments were the only places where I could relax. During showings, I stole keys. Afterward, I stalked anyone who wanted the rooms I chose for myself.

The crowds in the cities made me realize how different I was physically. Having seen so many people's bodies, I touched my own in the dark. For one thing, I had pen-stab perforations in place of nostrils. My profile was as flat as a mask's. For another, I seemed to have three lips. Doctors might have described the middle one as a strip of epithelial tissue that connected only to the sides of my mouth. I had a habit of pressing my tongue against it until it bulged, and worried that it might come loose when I wasn't trying to make that happen.

Worst of all, I had no discernible sexual traits—no beard or pubic hair—and my voice was helium-high. Sometimes I believed that Father wanted me to forgo puberty. That he'd surgically removed my parts, only to be murdered before he could return them. In other versions of that past, he never intended to give them back.

I felt less threatened living in larger cities because people were more tolerant. I explored condemned tenements until the possibility of dying in a collapsing building no longer appealed to me. Bored with moribund neighborhoods that were transforming like chrysalides into mechanized tourist hosts, I took a train to Chinatown and kept walking until the niceties of consumerism fell away.

No all-night delis or drug stores, no wine bars, no gastropubs. The only identifiable features were streets so bone-forlorn they seemed hypogeal. Storefronts that closed after lunchtime. Processions of darkened edifices. A mile or so later, huge dumpsters replaced trashcans.

I waited to see what would happen. Nothing did, so I fell asleep on some concrete steps.

After sunrise, the sidewalks became arteries clotted with bodies. A tourist holding a map called that area the financial district, though it was clear that people with money lived elsewhere. The transactions I witnessed involved cappuccino and muffins.

Then I saw a realtor's sign advertising a room in a residential building. The room didn't feel like a residence. Open house, read the sign on the door to the cellar apartment. I scoped the place out and moved in.

The first things I noticed about the interior were the little windows near the ceiling. They lined the living room wall that stood on the left as I entered through the hallway. Open curtains flowed from them all the way to the floor as if they did, too, and weren't as rectangular and narrow as granny glasses. Even though I rarely needed to hide, their position helped me to feel safe.

For decades, I lived in the place I found that day.

*

Sometimes I got sick of being alone and just started walking—usually toward the postmodern hotels that rose like hornet hives from the ribs of Chinatown. Between my place and that place, I lingered in shrinking slums.

The vagrants never lifted their heads when I walked past their slime temples at 20th and Pershing, asses braced against milk crates in candlelit teepees of dark green tarp. They rocked cross-legged in oil-flattened beards and bloodstained T-shirts with slogans like *Gone Crazy—Back in 5 Minutes*.

They wore expressions of indifference but managed to glance at everyone who passed except me. I reached down to try to misalign the elbow of a man whose lack of awareness seemed especially offensive, but his arm slipped through his sleeve and his flesh turned into vapor.

No bowtie'd maître d' from a failing hotel tried to solicit my business as his tuxedo-gloved fingers crawled along my arm. Every pedestrian stared ahead at some expected obstacle or down at some small mirrored rectangle.

An obese woman with wadded hair, and a cough that belied months of sleeping in the park, pressed her shoulder against the window of Peck and Quill, the only bookstore café in the city. She ignored me as I stood outside and pointed at her pile of damaged paperbacks. I thought she hadn't sensed my stare until I twisted toward the next intersection and felt her gaze shift slightly.

A crow croaked I am in the wine-hoarse voice of

an infant Dionysus. I could hear its declaration of identity. Why couldn't it see mine?

The Labrador on the other side of the street should have yawped in canine Morse code as I approached. He didn't sound that alarm. Instead, he chewed at his fur, his stare pivoting between his own ass and the swing doors of the supermarket behind him. He looked unconcerned by my proximity—which he must have known by smell—as if I'd been leashed to the parking meter and he was free. I decided to pour ipecac syrup on his paw. The queasy candy taste would turn into something else, reminding him who wore the collar.

Passing the storefront gate of a closed-down thrift boutique, I peered in and focused on this: A tiny spider millimetering its way along a crosshatched window screen until it saw me and stopped. It changed direction and began crawling toward me: an eye that was all black pupil using its lashes to travel.

Gnats and mosquitoes landed periodically as I stood in front of the gate. I shivered them off and continued through post-Chinatown. The penumbras of monoliths changed with my approach, sprouting flourishes and pink and green awnings. They glittered for me like fancy dinosaurs.

*

If I could visit a hospital and be seen by a bubble boy taped to his breathing machine, he might gasp this sentence to me through zippered cellophane:

Some people . . . would pay for . . . your kind of . . . anonymity.

This would be my counter:

That's what they think they want.

People who are jaded enough to pay to be faceless must have enjoyed physical contact with other humans once. They retain memories of intimacy that allow them to be wistful about isolation, whereas I could never imagine anything else. I can't reject what I've never been given any more than I can stop wanting what no one has offered.

No one except the scuttling blister beetles.

*

By four o' clock, the walkways darkened and no one chose to loiter. Windowgates lowered. I switched on my penlight and tilted my head, imagining how my misshapen reflection might stretch across the glass. I turned to watch the others leave, which felt better than walking beside them until they recoiled without realizing why.

I wanted to trace the contours of their suits with my fingertips. I wanted to lick their lapels. Their abandonment of the vicinity and, by extension, of me allayed my craving so that I could focus on the pothole next to the crosswalk where I stood.

Nearly everyone who worked in the area lived somewhere else after four. The office complexes and specialty shops that surrounded them closed promptly before sundown, as if people were embarrassed to be seen working late. No subordinate wanted to be caught strolling past a storefront or boom gate after the stockbrokers had deserted it. Not even tailors or waitrons were humble enough to stay.

It was nine o' clock by the time I made myself walk home. Even then, I didn't rush, since my surroundings now existed only for me. The spreading dusk painted Hambleton shadowcrowds everywhere. No fluorescent lamps exsanguinated the intersections with their bloodless pallor; the path stayed richly black. Alleys and side streets relied on the moon for illumination. Where copses of skyscrapers conspired to occlude lunar transients, I switched on my flashlight reluctantly. So that, after ten, when the highest windows of Le Corbusier clones were the last source of lambency, my separation from the world felt chthonic. Somewhere in the charcoal dark, a man lay on the street smoking a cigarette and gesticulating, his zigzags in glowing ash like a child's with an orange sparkler. He didn't see me, either—not even when I held my flashlight like a club and raised it over his head.

*

Demimoth

The first time a moth kissed me, I stood at the end of a pier promenade overlooking a river crowded with ghost ships. The creature air-swam into view and bussed my neck. Being kissed by it meant that suddenly I could be seen by them: Two middle-aged men who stared at me absently whenever I looked up. It was my first time being visible and I hated it. I didn't want to watch myself be watched. I could feel my dead mother's heart fist at the sense of it—the antennae exploring me through my windbreaker—but then the heavens rent. Sensing my thrill of discomfort, other moths fluttered around us until, shielded, we rose: Lifted by breath and burr as the promenade shrank below us.

*

Now I turned the last corner and, past the silhouette of the groundskeeper, made out light behind the glass doors of the façade. My building was an anachronism with nothing welcoming about it. The owner called it the Luxuman. That name, set in an Old English font and cast in aluminum, appeared just below its maroon-painted awning. It established a tone of ostentatious quaintness that was intended to attract a doddering class of tenants.

Once in, I took the elevator even though I lived on the basement floor. I wanted to feel catered to by someone and my someones were mostly machines.

The only voices in my apartment were the radiator's gurgle and the whirring of the fridge. I sat down and stayed there, drinking the windowdark.

*

Long gossamer drapes imitated the sounds of the crawlers who watched me. Fan-blown veils of flayed ether scraped against the edges of an old cardboard box. Whenever I stopped paying attention, the scrape became an arrhythmic chitter. It alarmed me only because I couldn't predict the timing. Silhouettes of molting pincers snipped the air. I sat motionless until the squeaking floor made me twitch; abruptly, mandibles clicked like camera shutters. I'd awakened the blindsighted things that creaked all around me.

*

A few times a week, I heard sounds from another kind of tenant: Stabbing laughter through plaster, one-sided conversations, thumping EDM. All of it emphasized the suffocating compass of my space, just as the bluish edges of silhouetted folding chairs underscored the lack of company.

This time, I could hear my nearest neighbor whooping through emerald-speckled darkness, then the three syllables he repeated while attempting to interrupt someone on his headset: *If you knew . . . if you knew . . . if you knew. . . .* Then a slap against the wall and the word *fuck!*

Fasteners snapped open, followed by the scrape of a pick slide and a wooden knock that meant he was doing the thing I dreaded. He hesitated and overtones of silence droned I was safe until he strummed his hollow-body electric and whined the one song he knew, his stumbling thrum of bar chords muffled and amplified simultaneously by the wall between us. He wouldn't stop pressing the headstock of his plaything against the jar in which I lived.

I lay down on my floor mattress oily with pore-wept fluids that cloyed like the leavings of my visitors. Every spore and organism in the building willed him to stop until he did and I grabbed the bat I stole for this one purpose: To test the wall and awaken the things behind it.

I tamped down the filth in the holes in the plaster, brandishing the bat shakily and clutching at violet scotomata until a few glistening inhabitants emerged. I couldn't see their eyes, compound or simple, or discern the color of their exoskeletons. I could only smell the sweetblood of their stimulation.

Imagine hearing the rustling and flakefall as they moved behind the plaster. Imagine following their shapes, first as bulging reliefs that formed huge radials across the walls and then as severed talons once they emerged: darkening and darting, prolegs skittering with each tap of the bat. Stucco reliefs and barbed inkspills like shrines to Earth's first inhabitants.

The kinetic Rorschach dripped toward me, stippling and spraying the walls around me: silverfish and leaproaches, termites and bone-house wasps.

The red worms that appeared last made me suspect that an upstairs neighbor had left behind a carcass that offered a complete food for the hackled mesh weavers that I'd somehow brought from Father's basement. I felt slightly jealous thinking about that: Another man.

First their chitter and slither, then the tickle of

their extremities on my arms and ankles. The burn of their bite patterns descending my arms as the ankle stings traveled higher. The flutter of burrowers. Feather-exquisite feelers tracing sites to be revisited by acid-wet mouthparts.

Swarms of devotees caressed my skin until, like the plaster around me, it rose in patterned welts.

"Close your eyes and let it happen. Relax and close your eyes."

*

I am preceded and succeeded by darkness because I am a disturbance within the darkness. Strangers feel the breath of my company when the afternoon ends and the glare of the sunlight is gone.

I am preceded and succeeded by darkness because I am a disturbance within the darkness. Strangers feel the breath of my company when the afternoon ends and the glare of the sunlight is gone.

I'm never inside you until you sleep, but I'll always be waiting nearby.

The same is true of leaproaches. When the light returns, they spring away, only to slide into crevices in the floorboards and sheetrock around you, leaving your skin slick with their visits, your nerve ends tickled by feelers that are no longer there.

The insects never had trouble finding me in the dark. No gaslights conducted them through my hallways, no north star pulsed through the gloaming to guide them. Only the dimmest glow in the toxin-occluded sky suggested I existed at all. But within that site of my shunning—the murk that precedes and succeeds me—they sensed that I lay awake; that my nerves broadcast my receptiveness to contact. My scarred arms were their touch-map, their cartography of sites of reproduction.

I recognized their vicinity by a faculty that is often miscast as intuition. No doubt you're familiar with the smell of garbage cans in the stairwell of a tenement. But if you had no sense of smell, you would come to recognize the *proximity* of garbage.

Everyone knows how it feels to wear a T-shirt that hasn't been washed in weeks. At first, you feel the cloying of the oil-infused cloth. If you keep wearing it, the shirt chafes the skin until, at last, bumps rise to describe the travel of the fabric.

When you're unable to smell it, trash makes the surrounding air *feel* like rancid sugar. The insects' proximity could feel that way as well.

They buzzed when they flew but also when they landed. The whirr of their wings, their dive-bombing shrieks, described the contours of my face.

*

It became a habit to try to decode the patterns of hurt on my skin. Did they mirror the shapes of oak branches in the coppice by the window or were they an expression of something less mimetic? For ages, I couldn't decipher their meaning though I knew their complexity was compulsive. Fixations hid in those rigidly busy designs.

Rows of welts described my body like trellises of purple vines maintained by an obsessive gardener. They limned it as distinctly as hatching lines in an etching. Second veins, I called them, veins painted over the veins beneath. Squid tentacles with the flesh stripped away so that their convolutions trailed like trickles. Hokusai studies of knotted waterfalls.

*

One Saturday night, I tried walking to the bathroom but found I could only stumble. I barely made it back to my mattress before exhaustion flattened me and I angled into my spot under the tangles of blankets. I couldn't get warm enough. I turned and so did the room and when the cycle finally stopped, I lay nauseous and furled in a newspaper cocoon. Multiple

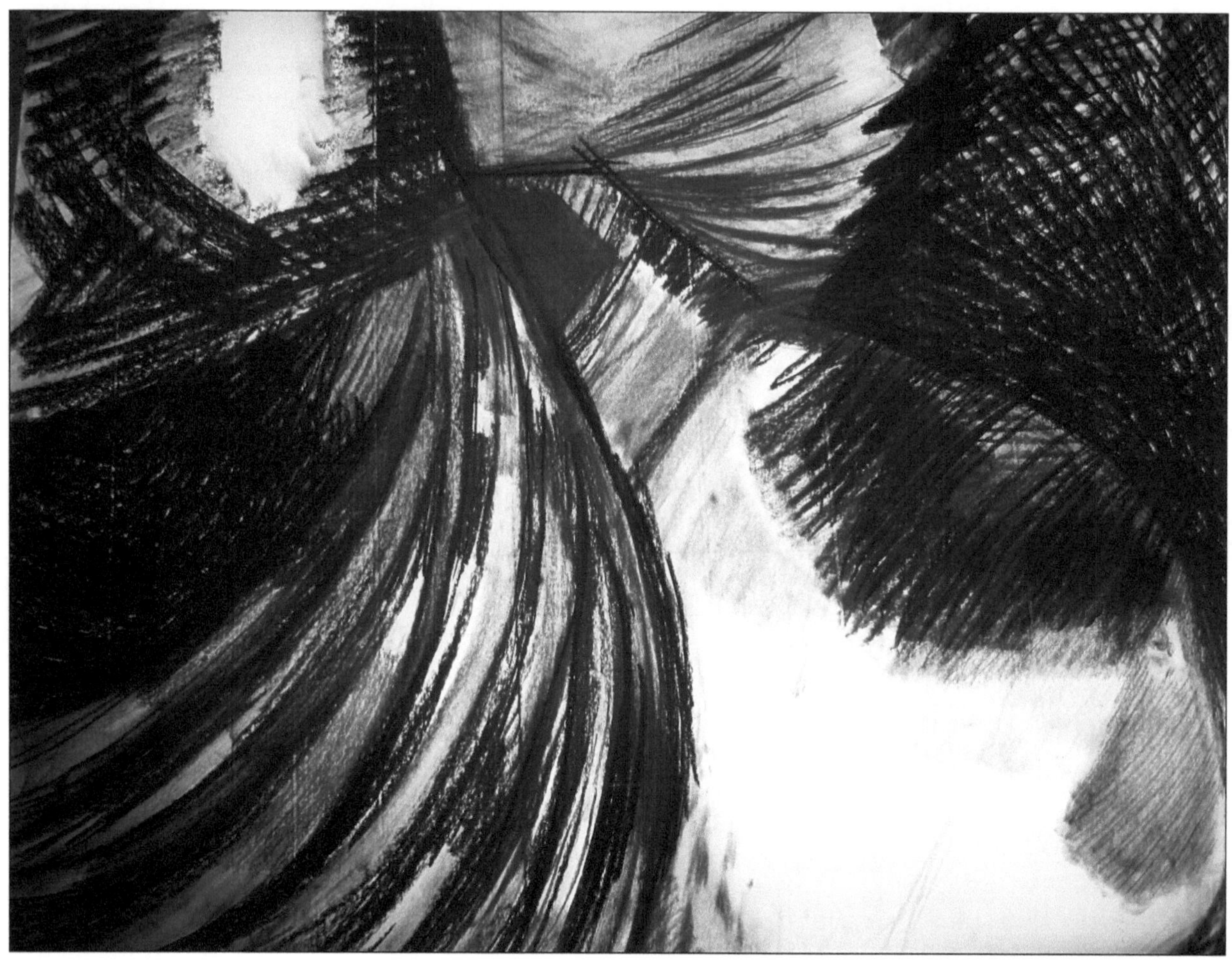

Abstract in Gray #1, charcoal on paper drawing by Leslie Hardie

images of the blue-black hallway wheeled in the dark like salvia petals, slowing until they merged.

Just above my bed: a window too icy to close, the blind lowered and flapping against exhalations like negatives freckled with snow.

I tried not to shiver and lay still, welcoming the fever. Only the twitch of its ministrations revived me occasionally: The tightening of the triple-cruciform embrace of its six jointed legs.

In a few days, I was able to hold a book, but even reading depleted me. I couldn't follow the logic of an essay after focusing on it for more a few moments. I tried propping a tablet between my hand and elbow to watch a movie but kept dropping it on myself, awakening with the impact each time until I slid it next to my pillow.

Soon I was dreaming about hornets made of shreds of 16mm color film. They flew at me and attached themselves to my face, where they wheeled transparent stingers on thorax discs over my eyes. We projected the frames of hornet shorts against cloud-banks by means of my incandescent retinas. My white pupils served as strobes with focusing lenses.

Weeks later, I awoke staring at a blur that sharpened into a flatbug on the windowsill. The tiny thing resembled a larger species that had ridden me for years. It lay dead on its back, legs folded, as if waiting to be placed in a hibernation locket, its body the color of rusted brass. The edges were ridged so that, when I flipped it on its legs, it looked like one of the centuries-old arrowheads that Father said he found just beyond our backyard. Its eyes still reflected the presence of the one who had stopped them.

I couldn't remember standing upright even once in the previous weeks, let alone having the strength to move things around. But somehow, the window was closed and the room felt warmer; the rug, dry beneath my feet.

I edged the bug into a ziploc bag for research. Before sealing it in, I stopped to look again: pummeled metal affixed with the mask of a sun god's face.

The sight of it reminded me of my afternoon with a hive of cuckoo wasps and I got excited thinking about the luster of their iridescent-blue bodies. Normally, I could have pictured them in eidetic detail. This time, it felt as though my brain had been replaced with dense gas. The images glazed over like frost on a windshield, like misted cracks in place of clearer forms.

I tried to see them until I couldn't stand up any more. I had to drop onto the mattress on my stomach before the windup key in my back stopped completely. I landed in a graceless position with one elbow digging into my calf. I tried to spread my arms but soon realized I couldn't move.

I could feel my limbs softening and stretching until the skin began to tear. I tried to touch my elbow with my other hand but felt metal bristles there instead of fingers. My ribs were as brittle as shells and the shells were cracking.

*

As my body changed, so the onset of their company became subtler. I couldn't take my bat to the walls anymore, but they didn't need to feel it. They arrived when the shadows on stucco flowed into the hallway's hollow, obliterating the outlines of furniture in the Prussian-blue gloom. Perhaps I only dreamed that I could see them. Differences between walls and space dissolved like musculature made of licked rice paper.

I knew they were next to me by the sounds they made when they changed. If I turned on the night-light too quickly after it was over, the sight made me gasp before they fled, the image of their bloodied exoskeletons imprinted in my memory.

My gore was their rotogravure.

One evening, I switched on the light and they didn't flee, so I forced myself to look closer.

Hornets wore gelatinous masks that resembled faces from famous paintings—the eye and mouth-holes stretching and distorting as their fistheads pivoted—with black antennae for ears and white mandibles for teeth. Each had its own expression and rubbed its walking legs characteristically.

Feeding on my anomalous body for generations had caused them to mutate. I expected they might be larger than before, but not as large as gharials.

They inspected me hesitantly, as if stymied by the lack of design in my self-injuries. Even though I was still young, they made me feel like an old boardroom gentleman. Feelers grazed my shoulders as they spat cobalt powder on my chest, then skittered away. I stared at the ceiling and expected to study it for hours.

Something in the kitchen broke a dish and hit the floor with a clatter. Three sets of legs clicked against the tiles; a hexapod wearing taps. I lifted my head and saw what looked like a gargantuan bone-wasp in the hallway. It didn't care about being seen in the light. I recognized the face of Goya's Saturn on the taper of its long horizontal skull, and a place for an offering at the top of its head, which was flat like the seat of a bicycle. Like my other visitors, it held me in a swallowing stare. The aureole of its wings trembled as it swiveled its neck to challenge my squint. I could just make out the U-shaped pattern of spines on the back of its thorax, the sucking hairs on its walking legs and the deflated poison sac dragging behind it. Past visits taught me that an insect's stinger looks even more obscene when emptied. Although I'd been visited by its species hundreds of times before, I had to look away when the Saturn Bone-Wasp changed. What I'd mistaken for its face was a pattern of camouflage.

It hovered over my body, then dropped toward the edge of the room where I stood watching, which was when I realized that my shell lay elsewhere. I'd left my husk on the mattress and *it still saw me standing*.

I reached down to touch my arm with my fingers but could find neither fingers nor arm.

Saturn explored the fumes that had been my flesh and drove its stinger through my floating nervure. It clung to my wisps, released its venom and I shrieked gas. I was mist that could be molested. Its stings continued to penetrate me even though I flowed differently each time, a river that can't be fouled the same way twice.

I'm changing color, I thought. My blood turned to shreds of cloud.

Its walking legs vomited etheric sacs that glittered and rippled as they drifted in my scarlet fog. I sparkled in time as they moved through me, a misted glimmer.

As the rest of Saturn grew, its stinger shrank. It scuttled through me toward the hallway, where it paused to sneer again. Then it clattered off to its nest and left me to complete my transformation. I was pain that floated, cicatrices that opened to nowhere.

*

I never thought that my orgiasts would desert me until they did. What I presumed to be our relationship was only a site of sustenance meant to provoke a series of molts.

Certain insects can react symbiotically to changes in their host. In my case, they modified the function of my camouflage, effecting my phylogenetic transformation. They triggered my morphology, releasing the energy of the unformed part of me, only to retreat after completing the cycle. I stayed oblivious to that process because I chose to believe something else: That they were lonely and wanted to enjoy my body.

That would have been impossible for them. I see that now.

The decades inflict a tyranny of repetition. Eventually, actions become habits, which are then enshrined as rituals, which impose a reflexive and formulaic itinerary on everyday thoughts. So that removing one's glasses before bed feels the same as slipping off rubber gloves after an autopsy of the same cadaver, year after week, tenure after shift.

Strange, that there should be music to routine; a lilt to the refrain of the mechanics of despair. I can hear it whenever an elderly person strokes the face in a framed photograph, or a widower lays out his suit on his bed before work, or a soldier places the barrel in her mouth or presses the sword to her sternum.

I seemed consigned to such a suicide until my rooms became entirely aphotic, releasing me from internal lights and allowing me to thrive in dying.

*

I wouldn't have dreamed the insects would return to me after I passed. I assumed that death would seal me off with an inviolable signet. But the things that mystics claim to know are untrue. Emerson asserted that no one ages; that our energy survives without changing. If only. No matter. Experience proves otherwise. The ghost-parasites I've met were either dying or already dead. The manifestations of age are different for a disembodied being than a physical one, but they're equally apparent to insects. No one told me that my etheric form could be shredded and recast by ectoparasites as thoroughly as my former brain and skin.

This lesioned wisp of a vessel resembles the rooms it occupies: a space that is destined to be rented someday by someone else. I'll haunt it out of habit or diminish to nothing's dust.

*

Vagrant cinders of sunlight thin through the window; through an organdy curtain that must have been hung by someone else. It swishes and hisses like the train of an agitated bride. At 7:48 p.m., only the faintest periwinkle tinge remains visible behind the silhouettes of buildings. Lights flicker on in the upper windows of the complex, which loom brighter now than the sky my sentience has replaced. The room fluxes and refluxes, the ebb and flood of shadows around me synchronized to the breath of my beloved. I look down at my vanishing suckers and hooks, quivering like a spermatozoon because *someone* has rented the apartment and that someone is a gorgeous specimen of flesh.

For fun, I decide to perfect my mental map of my new host. I can't have all of him yet, but I feel like enjoying a snack. I won't be voracious until later, but exploring is foreplay. And nibbling, after all, is something to do.

The Calf

D. James Smith

Child of a dying wind it lay
In the muck and hot, blond grass
Below the dam and its strangled creek
That my boyhood friend and I
Crossed that morning, determined
To flee the nun's black habits and ink,
To claim all property, posted or not.

And I remember thinking the eyes,
Pulled by crows and gone, might have
Envisioned a wilderness complete.
I knew dogs could dream; why not cattle?

The flies under its tail, too furious
To be waved away, seemed to be trying
To tunnel up under the tail where coyotes
Had, most likely the night before, though
Not far enough because the creature lived.

Pete, who carried on his back the welts
Of his father's belt, had a near perfect ear
For silence, and so my best friend, this time
Threw back his head and made some kind
Of unholy screech, voicing the quarrel
The animal could no longer make.

My own throat bubbled with vomit
As if from that sink hole
When I plunged, then walked
The dull blade of his pocket knife
Up the corded artery of the neck.

We sat there half a lost afternoon,
Quiet, not understanding, yet,
How we'd chosen to love
What God would not.

Love and Strangulation

Carl Watson

THE PHILOSOPHERS OF THE OLD ROMANCES say, and many specialists today concur, that desire is nothing more than the result of a necessary and continuous projection of the self into others; an unattainable wholeness is represented in an outside object, a body, or a soul. That it must be unreachable is both integral to the relationship and maddening. Some renounce the quest altogether and go shopping. Others retreat into darkness.

Those who monitor behavior in the mental hospitals of Uptown describe a phenomenon in which patients scratch words on their skin with their fingernails or sharp instruments. Some can even make brief defining messages or images appear via the power of the diseased mind alone. Locked away in their heads, relishing their solitude, they seek contact with the outside world, yet they touch no one.

> *Simply having the words "Born to Raise Hell" on your arm can change your life—you end up killing a bunch of nurses or stabbing your best friend in a card game because you somehow had a picture of yourself doing it.*

A more social, if trendy, alternative exists in the ancient tribal rite of tattooing. The very longevity of the tattooed image or mark, at first a choice, can, over time begin to seem as if it were prescribed, imposed, imprinted by outside forces. This may, of course, merely be buyer's regret manifesting as identity.

Bernadette had a friend who did tattoos at a place called Kaligraphy Studios on Broadway and Montrose. This friend, Marcus Boggs, claimed to be related to the banjo player Dock, although, unlike Dock, he had a strong mystical bent. He believed that the black tattoo ink was the symbolic blood of the Black Goddess Kali and, therefore his art was sacred because it mingled the blood of humans and gods. This idea was the origin of the studio name.

Boggs was in his twenties but looked older, due to his long black beard and signature style of dress, which was part low-rent rabbi, part 19th century snake-oil salesman. His favorite book was *The Illustrated Man* by Bradbury. He'd loaned it to Bernadette and one night came to get it back. Thus started a bullshit session with peculiar consequences.

Sophie was there and steered the conversation toward her interests—serial killers with romantic names: The Green River Strangler, The Mississippi Muskrat, The Sunnyside Slasher. She had just read a criminal case study about a guy from Texas known as The Red Spider. When they caught him, he claimed his homicidal anxiety was caused by the little red spiders tattooed all over his hands and arms—a kind of post-coital arachnophobia, *i.e.* after the fact. In any case, he eventually felt he was being attacked by his own skin.

There were lots of examples if you looked for them, Sophie said, of people getting trapped in a metaphor of their own design—bad poets, false gurus, bad lovers, megalomaniacal despots, etc.

Bernadette knew a story about a guy in West Virginia: a man who had thirty-seven butterflies tattooed on his body. He was called Butterfly Bob by the locals. He was also an artist and drove around in an old Ford pickup truck painted with Victorian fairies. Bob had a collection of small animals preserved in jars. He thought of them as babe magnets. And he was kind of

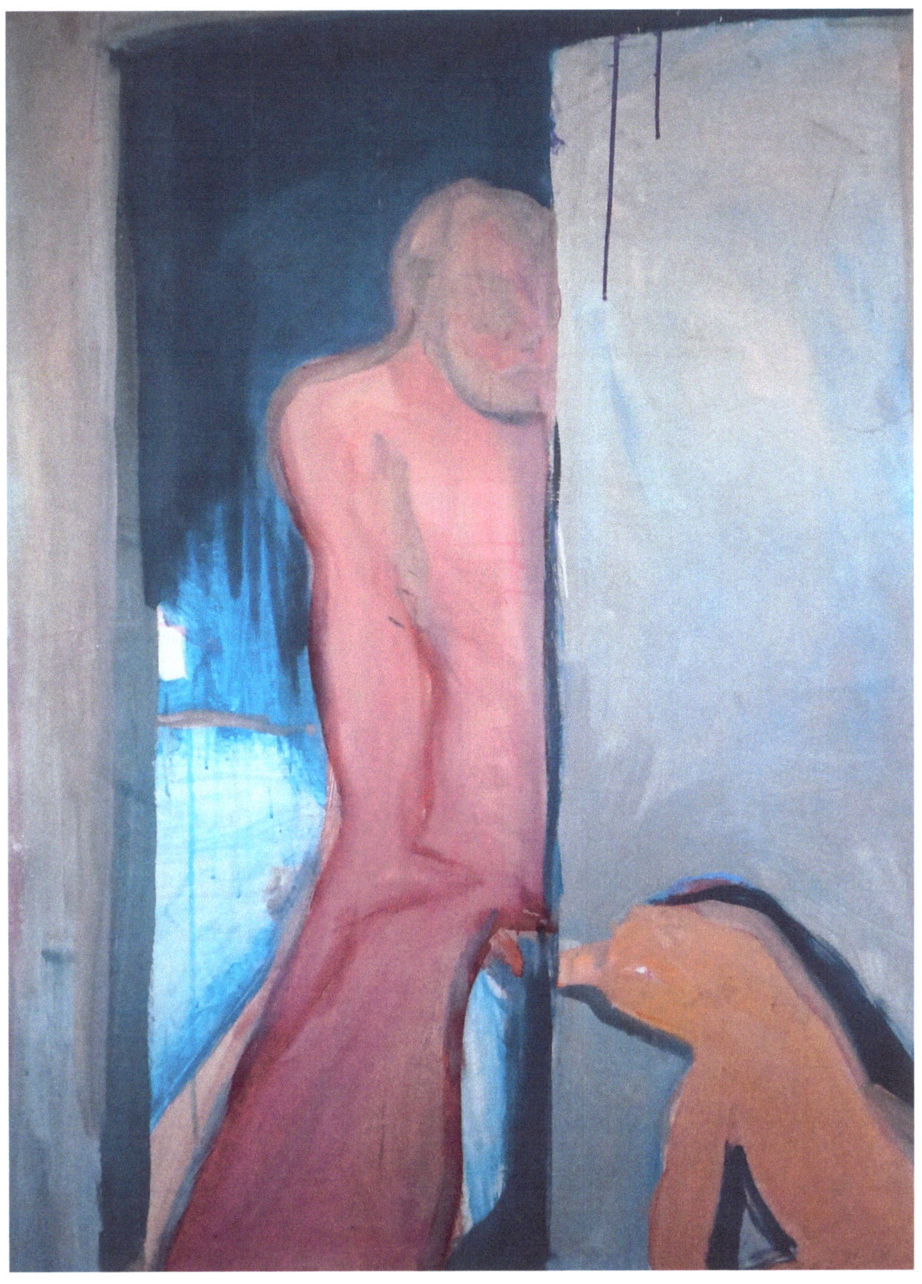

Crime in the Hallway, Acrylic and spray enamel on board, 36" x 48", 1984, by Stephen Lack

caretaker of a motel outside Madison. He met her in church and she gave him purpose. It turns out her family was from a small village in Michoacan, the central Mexican state where the Monarchs winter.

"See," Sophie said.

"See what?" I asked.

"See, we all end up victims in the end."

"Victims of what?"

"Of the little things—dreams, obsessions."

Boggs had a theory: tattoos were a lot like paranoia, he said—they begin as fantasies and end as fate. Simply having the words "Born to Raise Hell" on your arm can change your life—you end up killing a bunch of nurses or stabbing your best friend in a card game because you somehow had a picture of yourself doing it. The image becomes a dare forcing a bifurcation in your personal timeline. You can also look back and say it wasn't your fault: "the image made me do it."

handsome in a West Virginia way. In fact, he managed to pick up women at the local bar. The women were scared, of course, but they were also game. For a while they had the thrill of not knowing whether they'd be dead or alive when the night was over.

One day a gunshot wound from a jealous husband inspired a religious conversion and Bob began to court, and eventually marry, the aging Mexican

People will never stop baiting themselves forward through life with such ideas. "Eventually" in cosmic time becomes "inevitably." But the opposite is also true—events that actually should be expected end up being a surprise. You just don't know where you're at in the probability continuum.

Which brings me to the story of Robert Arno, which was a surprise because it turned out Boggs and I both knew the guy. The summer after high school, me and Arno were both flipping burgers at Johnson's Grill on Highway 41. Arno was just old enough to drink back then. He quit in the middle of his shift one night and got drunk with this guy Tim "Buck" Catertoe, or Timbucktoo as we called him. They often went to this motel bar across the road on their break. They met women there and sometimes didn't come back to work.

Timbucktoo eventually got fired. So did Ron Ugly. Ron was the guy who put the butcher knife through the kitchen side door for fun. There was a spate of firings that season. Spinner got fired, and Johnny Flange, two weeks earlier. I got fired myself. But this was all years ago. Then, in the early '80s, Arno turned up in the Lakeview neighborhood of Chicago. He and his mother had moved to Albany Park to be near their cousins after his dad died. But Arno quickly drifted east, drawn by what he perceived as bohemian freedom. He was the boyfriend of one of Berny's girlfriends, so he was sometimes at her place for parties.

Turned out Arno knew Boggs via Baltimore back in the day. And lately he'd been going by Kaligraphy to get some work done. It was a big job, full chest—some violent Hindu demon perched on a volcano with fire and fish spewing out of it. The volcano was ringed by skulls with worms winding through their eye sockets.

Arno also had, covering each shoulder, these sinister-looking swans whose wings seemed to form epaulets. Their elongated necks reached down the biceps, circling around and ending in toothy beaks a few inches past the inside elbow. Then on the inside of each wrist was the small black *Q* of a curled serpent. Arno called them the Nagas of Vedic mythology. The whole tableau had a sort of comic-book quality.

I only know all this because, one night at Berny's, the tattooed people got drunk and started taking off their shirts. After Arno left, I wondered out loud if his torso of violent cataclysm coupled with the Eastern mysticism symbolized a confluence by which he might eventually break on through to another side—a new and better man.

Shortly after that, Bernadette threw me out. She had to work the next day.

But it wasn't even a month later when she called: "You gotta come over, man."

"What?"

"Just come over."

When I got to her place, a few people were there. Boggs told his story. Apparently, a few days earlier, Arno came to his shop acting even weirder than usual—kind of irritable, distracted, and there was a noticeable tremor in his voice. Boggs didn't think much of it because Arno was so full of shit anyway and he was always over-dramatizing his emotions.

"So how's Stacey?" Boggs had asked.

"Gettin' on my nerves, as usual," Arno replied, pacing around.

"I know what you mean, man."

"No, really, I wanted to fuckin' strangle her this morning. I mean I just could not listen to her anymore." He said the word not with a certain finality. "I mean I love her but . . . but you know, I have a few drinks or something, I go hang out. So fuckin' what? She's always gotta be on my back."

Boggs tried to placate him. "Yeah, I know. I feel like killing Margaret almost every week. Funny thing is—she's still around. It's our fate man. You know the cliché. Can't live with 'em . . . ."

"Ain't no good dead either, I guess," Arno said, looking at the floor.

Then they had some beers and watched part of the Cubs game. That was a few days ago.

But here's the thing—just that morning, a friend found Stacey in her apartment on West Cuyler. She was naked on the floor, cold and blue with her tongue hanging out, looking very much broken and raped. Cops were asking questions. Arno was in the wind. Then Boggs remembered that tremor in Arno's voice, the emphatic "not," and said it should have been a clue.

Sophie got riled and blamed Boggs. She said maybe Stacey would still be alive if Boggs hadn't put all that ink on him, turned him into a freak. "Think about it," she said. Sophie was always a little hostile toward Boggs anyway. She thought he was pretentious.

Bernadette came to his defense. She said, "If you're

going to think that way, you might as well not speak either. For that matter, better not even get out of bed. There's no telling what sinister chain of events you will start just by your presence in the world. It's the anxiety of influence. It'll freeze you in your tracks."

Boggs just sat there looking worried.

Then one night about a week later, I got one of those "2 AM phone calls" that you know are bad news before you even answer. The phone seems to glow and your hand trembles above the receiver and you feel like you've entered a Hitchcock movie or something. I picked it up anyway, half asleep. It was Boggs, calling from his wife's house in Baltimore.

"What the fuck?" I said, a little irritated.

"I don't know man, I been thinking about this whole thing." He was talking sort of crazily but slow and deliberate.

"Well don't," I said. "Think about me, sleeping. I was sleeping, you know."

Boggs ignored me and went on. "I've become like a cameraman of my own future life, which plays out before me like some kind of strange experiment. What I mean is—there is no actual morality, there is only data that we receive, read, and act on. The mind computes, we make the story out of it later."

"Uh-huh," I said, not sure what he was getting at.

"I'm telling you, I'm not in it," he said, "I'm always a couple of steps behind. There's like this slight delay and it's been getting longer recently. If I keep going like this I'll be able to witness my own death and there will still be enough time left for me to . . ." He didn't finish the sentence.

"I feel that way myself most days," I said. I was being dismissive. "I think you better come back, man. It's not good to be alone."

He only got more adamant, "No, see. See, that's the last sadness: You realize—that if you had known all the time you could have changed things."

"Look, I don't know what you mean, but . . ."

He interrupted me again. "You know, I can kind of understand where Arno was coming from. God is happy despite the subtle crimes. The universe computes. Everything is on track."

As he spoke, I realized Boggs had an odd tremor to his voice, too, probably just exactly like Arno had a few weeks earlier. I started to imagine his wife's body on the floor, as if the murder scene was being replicated, splitting and growing like a cancer cell in the social imagination.

I asked about his wife. "How's Margaret? She all right?"

He didn't answer. Then I wondered why Boggs was calling me anyway. He was better friends with Berny.

"What's going on, man? You talk to Berny?"

"Yeah. Yeah. No, her phone was out. I'm fine. But listen, if you talk to her, tell Berny I'm OK. I'm not coming back though, not for a while." There was a voice in the background, a man's voice, a whining voice. It sounded familiar.

"Who's that?" I asked.

"I gotta go," he said.

"Yeah, all right. Sure." Silence.

I phoned Bernadette immediately. Contrary to Boggs's claim, her phone was working. I said I thought Boggs had gone off, and that maybe he even knew where Arno was, that he might be in communication with him. I didn't know for sure, but I had this feeling.

"He doesn't know." Her voice was anxious but quiet.

"What do you mean?"

"Because he's here," she whispered.

"What? Where?"

"He's on the couch, in the other room." She hung up.

The rest of the night passed in a blur of sirens and flashing lights, unwanted phone calls and anxious glances. Berny had told the cops, probably because she was afraid. Arno slept in holding that night. The rest of us drank but only got morbid. I ended up walking Sophie back to her apartment at about four in the morning. It was raining a little when we reached her building. In the streetlight, her skin glowed white and wet, like apple meat, contrasting with the red skin of her lips. Her hair lay flat against her head. It gave her that seductive gamin-like look which, for some reason, always triggered my savior complex. We were exhausted, depressed, stunned into submissiveness. She thought we should do something about the situation. I wanted to believe we could.

Fairies

Julia Kissina

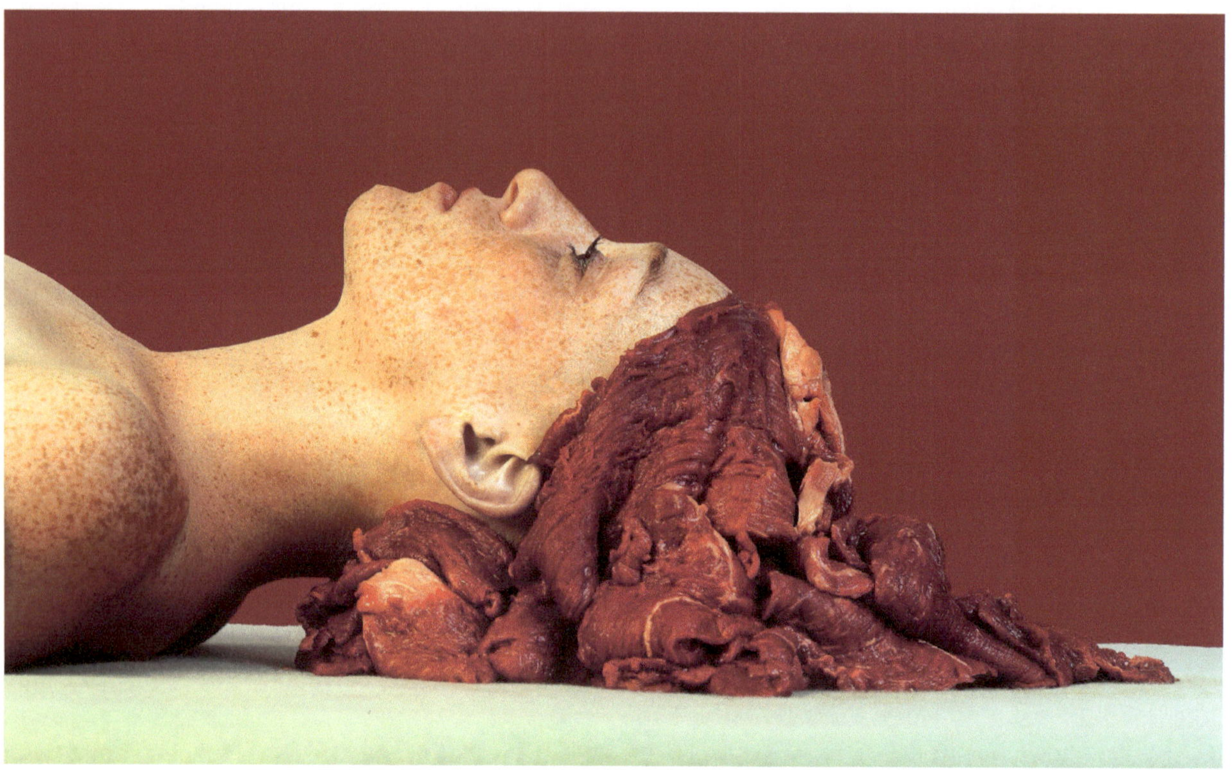

From the *Fairies* project, 1997–98, photograph by Julia Kissina

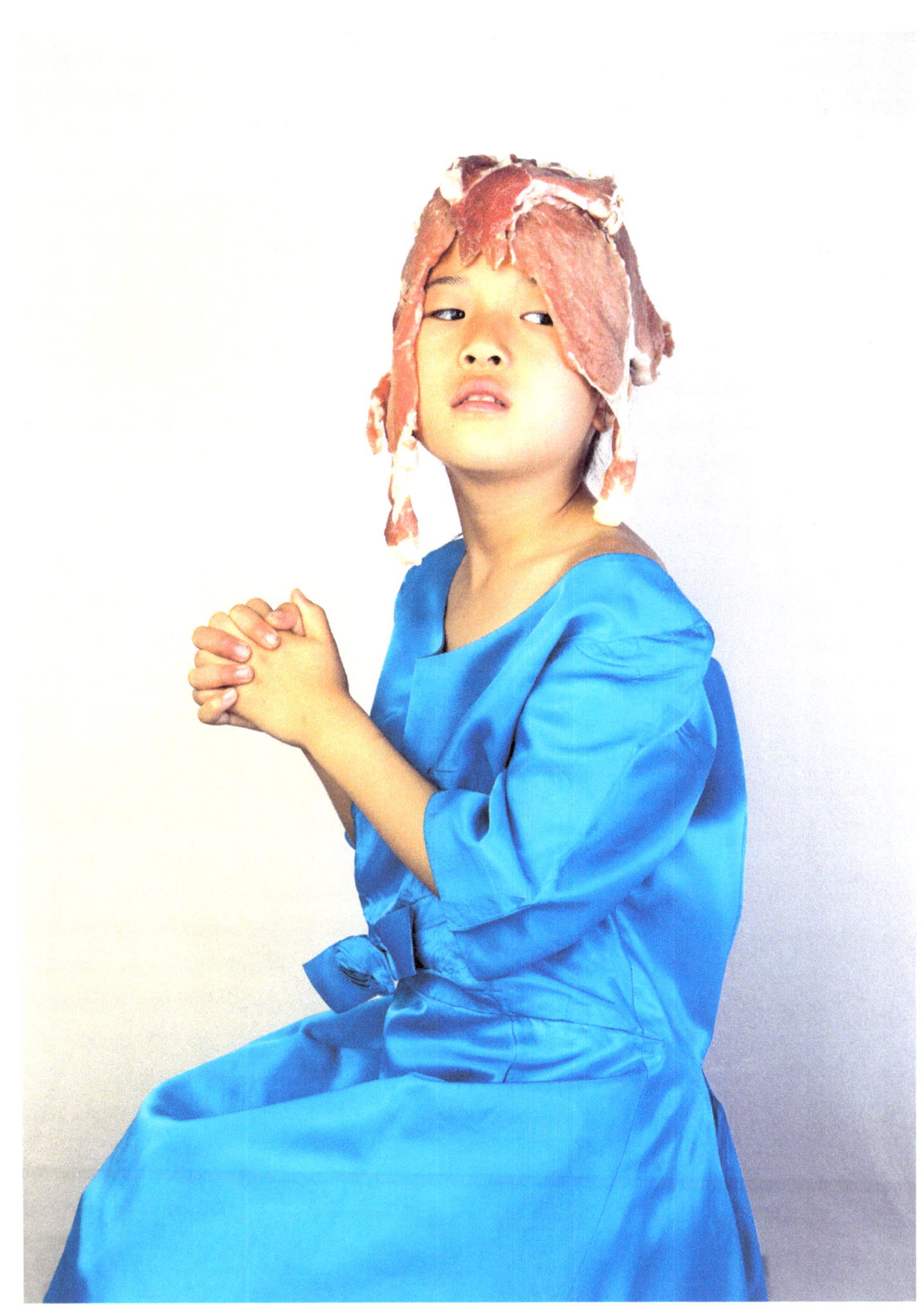

From the *Fairies* project, 1997–98, photograph by Julia Kissina

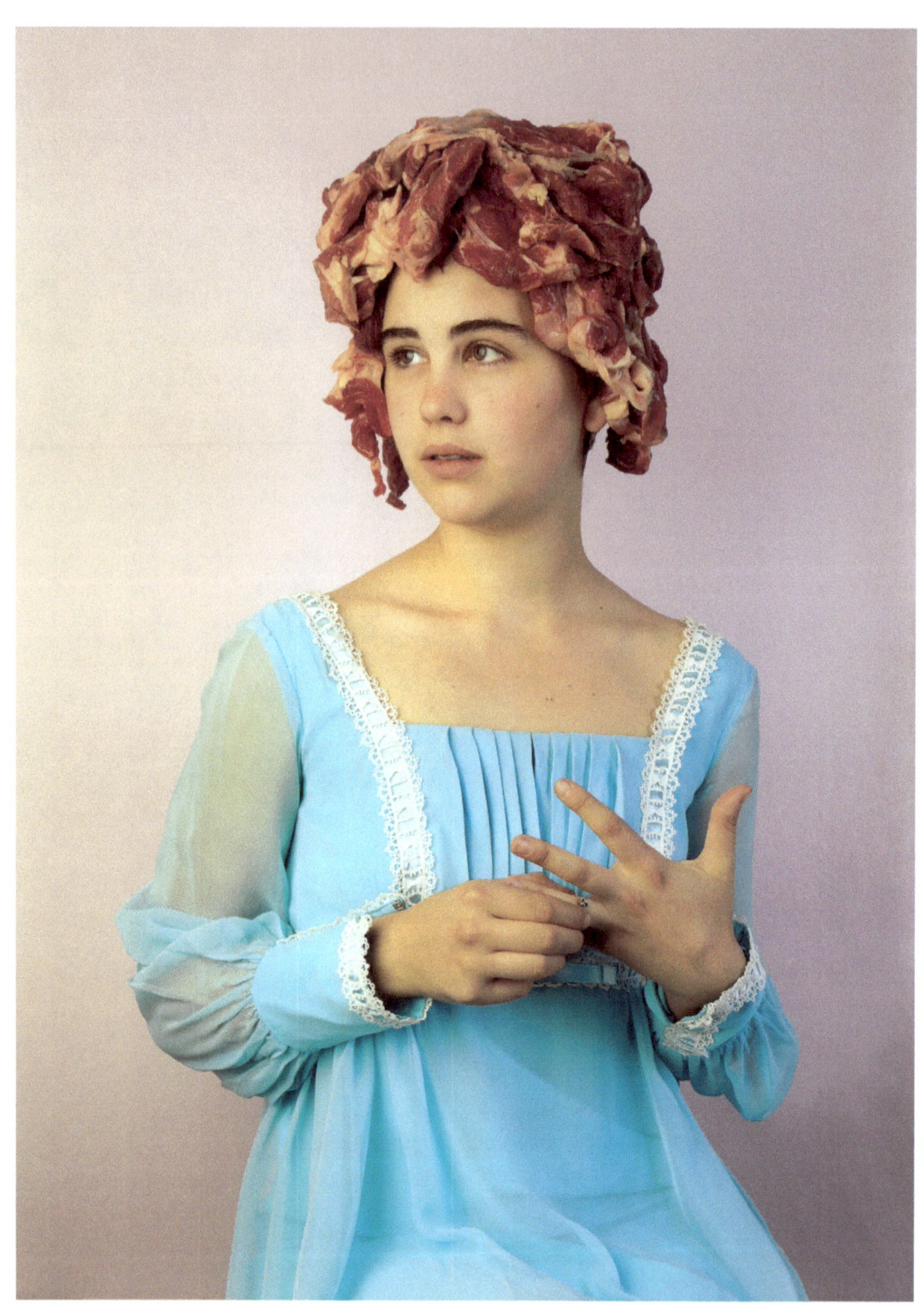

From the *Fairies* project, 1997–98, photograph by Julia Kissina

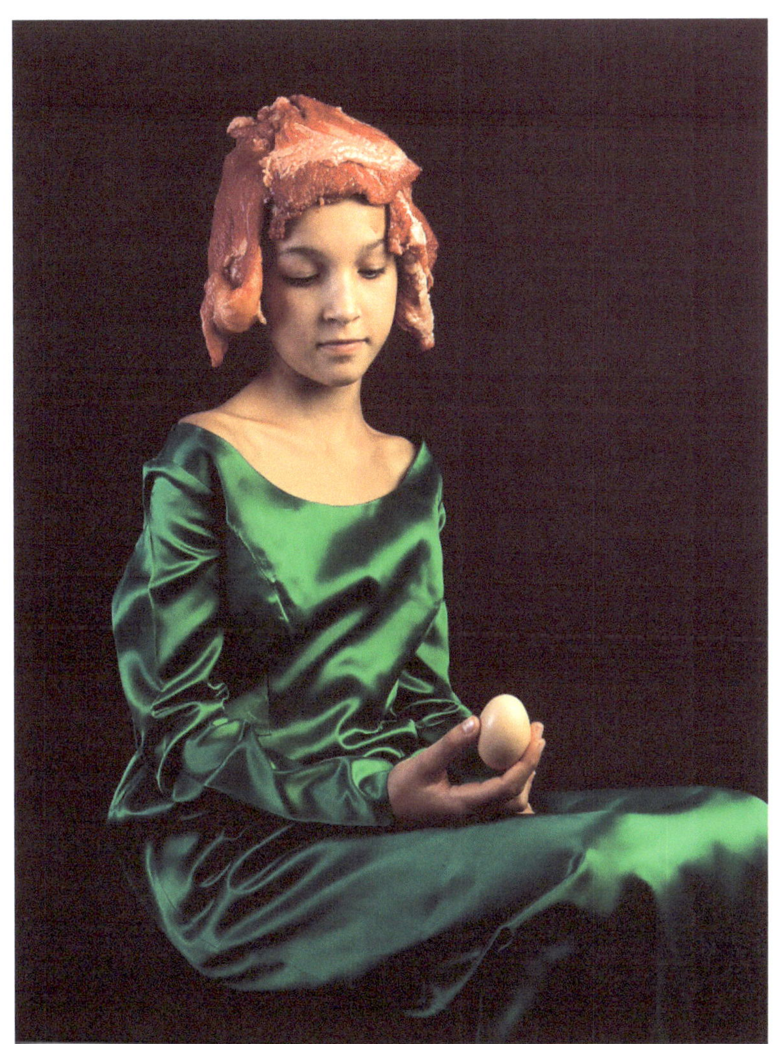

From the *Fairies* project, 1997–98, photograph by Julia Kissina

Santa Barbara-1980 / San Francisco-1982

Matt McClaren

Santa Barbara–1980

I didn't have a mattress yet. It had been three months, but I still lay in my room on my dirty clothes, arranged under a fitted sheet. Ron stood in my doorway, leaning against the jamb. He stared at me, idly picking at the skin on his chest underneath a red silk shirt. "So I need a ride over to the west side," he said. "What do you say?" I shrugged. "I need to cop, I'll give you a nice bump out of the bindle." I was hitching out to Vegas the next day for Eddie's eighteenth birthday and it would be cool to surprise him with some coke, so off we went.

In the car, Ron stared out the window talking half to himself, half to me. "This fucker . . . this fucker, man. He always shorts me, always, every time, never fails. Not by much but he does. He must think I'm a punk, thinks I don't notice but I do, I do man. I got a scale now and always, always he is point two or point three short. Always. Myra says he's probably just lazy and forgets to center out his scale but he's a professional. That's bullshit."

We wound through the streets into the west side. The houses got shabbier, kids out in the street played with sticks and Mexican ladies sat on their porches lording over their never-ending yard sales. By now Ron was angry, his voice was sharp and full of hate. "There is no way this fucker is getting away with this. He has no idea who he is dealing with. He doesn't know who I've walked the yard with, you know what I mean?" he said, his eyes filled with empty rage.

He motioned to me to pull over and told me to cut the engine. We sat for second, he exhaled a long breath and reached into his sock, pulling out a snub nosed nickel-plated revolver. "I'm going in there and I'm gonna blow that cheater's toes off and take his stash. Wait here." And he was gone.

Besides the Banda music spilling out of the Mexican bar down the street all I could hear was the blood pumping in my ears. "Go now, go now, Matt. This is bad. If he shoots this guy you are going to prison, if he kills him you are fucked." I sat and stared through the window at an ice cream vendor laughing with a customer on the sidewalk and wished I were him. "Fuck the coke, Eddie won't care, this is ridiculous." An older couple walked past looking into the car, wondering what this white boy would be doing over here. "Great, now there are witnesses, I've been identified so even if I leave now, I'll still go down. They've seen the car. Just sit tight, be cool. If you hear a gunshot, drive out of here as fast as you can, at least it's a chance."

Ron slid into the passenger seat, deflated and slumped against the door. "He wasn't home, let's go," he mumbled. We drove slowly back over to the east side. The swooshing in my ears disappeared. "We'll get him next time, brother," he whispered. "You can, not me!" I blurted, all the pressure from the last half hour compacted into four words. Ron cocked his head and looked at me. I could feel it but didn't turn. All he said was "Fair enough little man, sorry to jam you up."

The rest of the ride was silent. The sun strobed through the high palm trees, the breeze circled through the windows and I saw everything for the first time even though I had just seen it a half an hour before.

San Francisco–1980

The bed was small, an undersized single. I didn't know they made them like that. Sink in the corner. There was actually a bare bulb, too.

But I had a window, looking out over the roof one story down and, at night, a neon sign on the corner that reflected off the walls outside and turned everything in the room the color of orange sherbet.

I set my books up on the dresser, large cloth-covered volumes that looked good. The stories were crap, mostly manly adventure novels written in the fifties that you could buy for a dime at the library salvage. I'd read them all the previous month. It had been

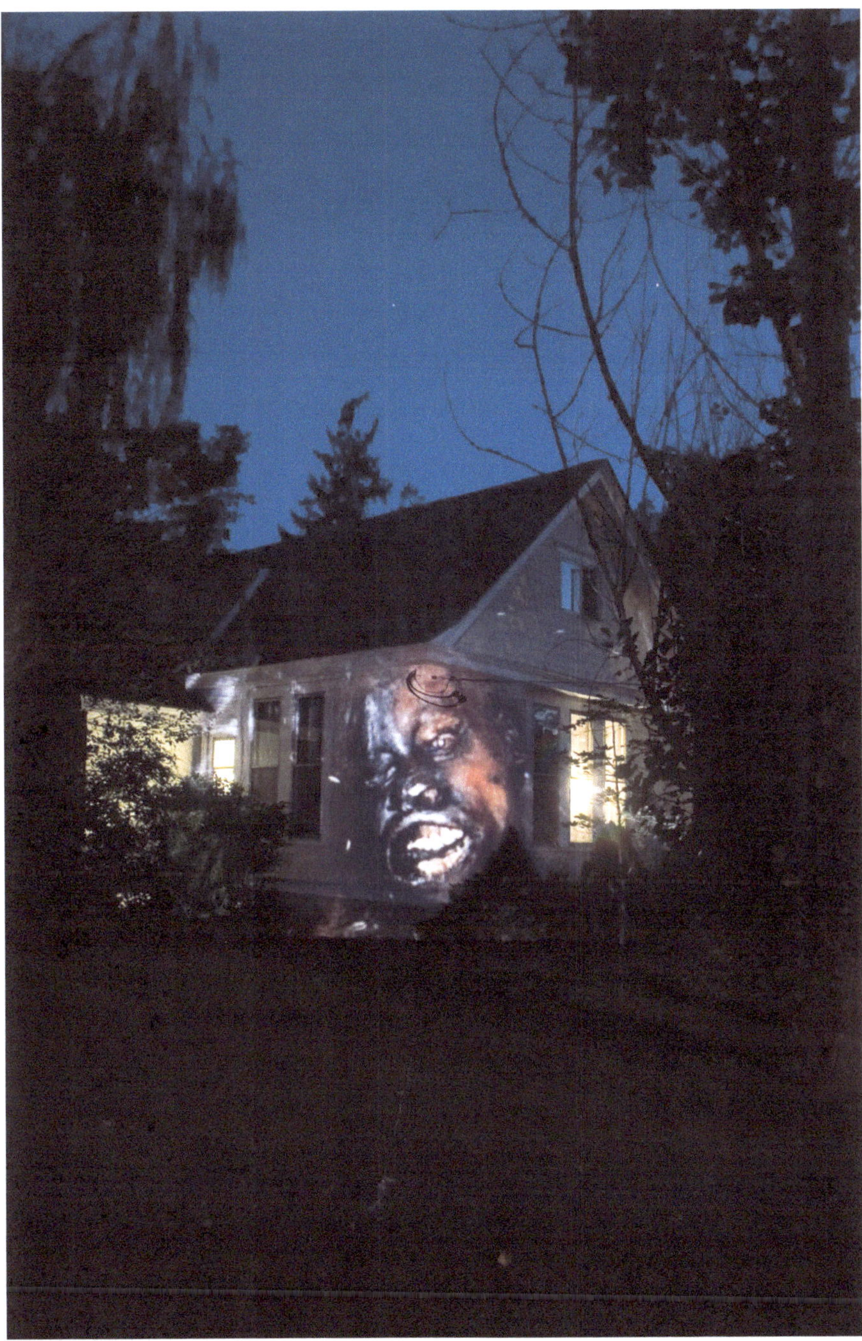
photograph by Jean-Christian Bourcart

and fuck. We could all hear each other and had abandoned the idea of dignity or privacy long ago, so making noise almost became a contest. Anonymous voices would holler out encouragement and taunts to an especially loud fight or fuck. Or sometimes there would be silence and everyone could hear the sounds bouncing off the buildings around us and back into our rooms. When the fighting or fucking would stop, applause and whoops would clatter up and down in sour slaps off the bricks. Screams of pain were always the favorite. Fucking was too common due to the clientele. One prostitute in particular was prolific, bringing in a new client on the hour every hour, like clockwork "That's right, work it daddy, you're built like a fucking horse." After a while, we would chime in with a chorus of horse whinnies when the inevitable line formed. After a couple of days someone yelled out. "For Christ sake, honey, everyone ain't Secretariat. Get a new line!"

peaceful. My routine was set: up by nine to get in line at St. Anthony's. Half of the men eating at the long tables never touched their coffee, so I would ask for theirs, pouring it into a large peanut jar.

Home with my jar, books and tobacco, sipping coffee heated up in my popcorn popper. It would get kind of rural in the afternoons, too hot to go out, so people stayed in their rooms to drink and fight

I had no place to go and didn't want or need one. But I did have a new volume of *Jim Talbot, Adventurer,* and he was going up the Amazon to set up a dredging operation for Conex. The sun was finally going down and my room was turning orange.

An excerpt from Toughboy, *a collection of stories.*

Beaches in Cornwall, Apples in Devon, A Foot in London

Christopher Romero

draped Kelp and no lullaby thick sound from deep wonder ritual unconformed
to sea sutra canters
the silver egg's path from studio
to rocks
near shore
to ocean soaked tidal pools lady lay day
heat mapped exposure turns sea weed to crimson in a dark room
near a far shore
where the mother's tongue's native father's melted in the pot
instead visions, moving lights
and nothing like spanish
back to the room
old pointed town beaches on both sides fine folks, ritual's child a bit of home there

The Apex Moralist and the Hot Birdman discuss the mineshafts
"Weird and Wonderful Devon Apples – Tom Putt, Slackmagirdle, Pig's Snout, Tale Sweet, Devon Crimson [not kelp!] and Oaken Pin to name a few"
Add another to the list
Tough Skin, oak's elegance, lofty output Name the woods, gentle the corners mind the man whose spine will fail him
spinning foam, gold flower headdress stacked two pound coins for Ganesha
know the hedges, peek rooms marked private alarms, chandeliers past Stag's den
mad dad, mind the last days, cost
in a mood is a continent
on this island one's vehicle rides best

The Mouth of the Dart seats conflicts free spirits from matters don't rhyme
curiosities, cabinets spawned through from the wigs to now
categories improved via theft, intrusion
reflection collection, Time's Keepers
Stone of tongues, action figures in 4000 years of marvel 10,000 years since sand put rites on the river
sound symbols make those rock tales
ur queen's gold flowers hearken to Devon
gong shields, flying horses, fine pair of Burma hmm should we keep the tridents?
the heads last retained body's own vehicle big foot in a sandal

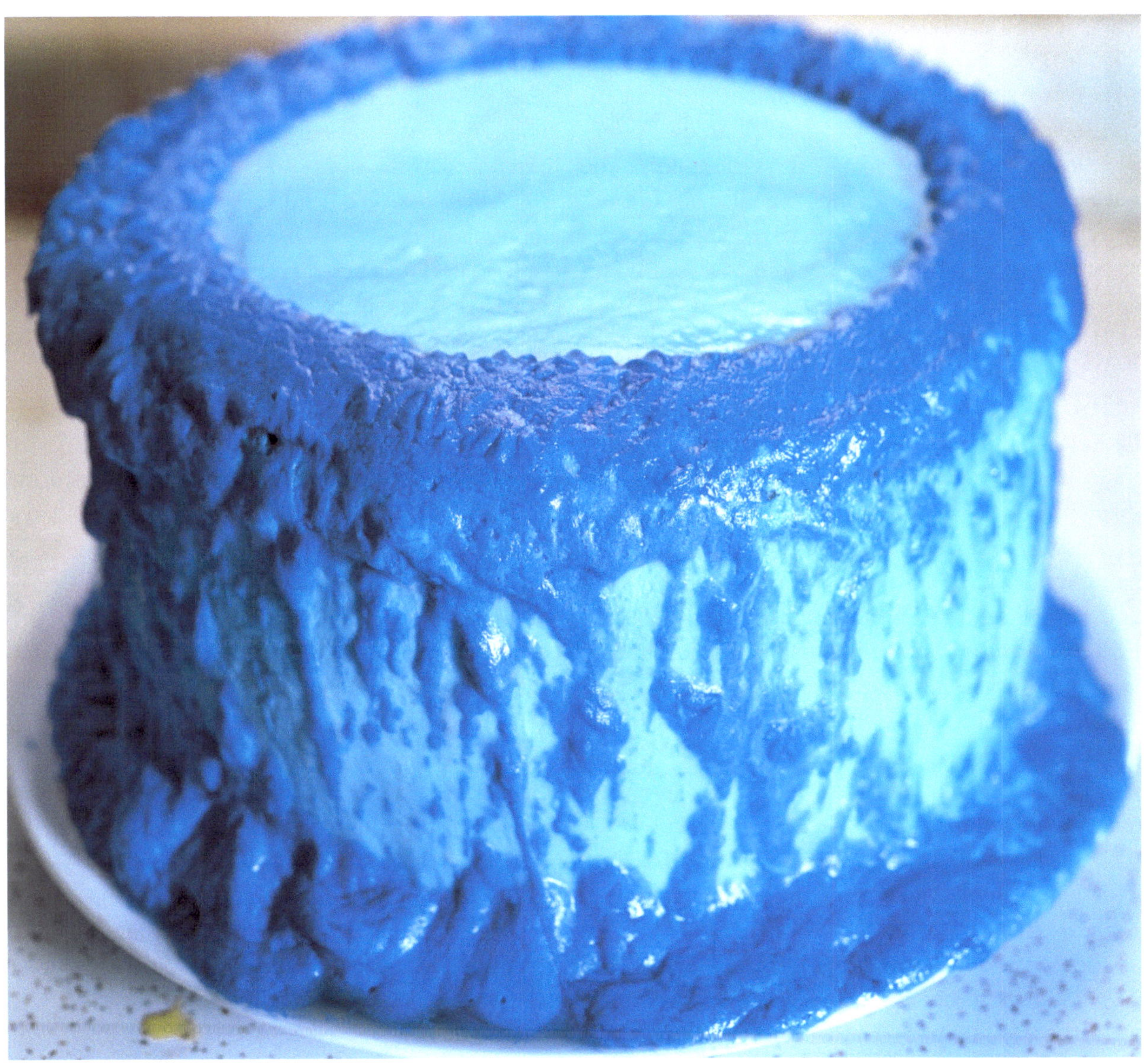

Erika, photograph by Dustin Wayne Harris

The 9 Lives of Ray the Cat Jones

Stewart Home

I'M A FACE. MY BREAKOUT FROM PENTONVILLE in 1958 has been praised as one of the greatest prison escapes of all time by the likes of south London gangster Mad Frankie Fraser. The details differ somewhat in the various accounts but here I'll put the whole thing together, just in case you can't be bothered to track down the lurid descriptions that have found their way into a slew of book and newspaper accounts.

It was a dark and wet winter evening with the London smog obscuring everything. Johnny Rider and myself were able to get onto the roof of the prison because it was being repaired and there was scaffolding going up the courtyard wall. The screws had been distracted by a disturbance I'd arranged to take place in the library class.

Johnny and myself made our way over the tiles and across to the sheer prison wall on the other side. Scaling down this almost impossible obstacle to my freedom, I smashed my right kneecap. Pain jolted through my body like an electric shock and I lost my grip on a windowsill and fell, breaking my left ankle. Rider coming down behind me clocked my mistakes and was able to make a safe descent. We then had to scale a second wall, and this time I broke my left leg as I jumped. Johnny, who was uninjured, made it safely to the ground.

Rider picked me up and tried to carry me from the prison wall to freedom, but I told him to leave me and get away. It would be better if at least one of us made a clean escape. Johnny ran, and because I couldn't run I crawled to a house door and asked the man who opened it if he'd help me. His wife came to see who was calling, and after telling her husband I was scary, she slammed the door in my face. I then made my way to a block of flats hoping to find somewhere to hide. I took the lift as far as it would go and then made my way onto the roof.

There was a skylight and, as I was trying to prise it open, I fell headlong through the glass and knocked myself out.

I was raised back to consciousness by flashlights being pointed at me. From the conversation going on around the smashed skylight above me, I could tell I'd been found by the authorities.

"Looks like he's dead." The screw's voice was emotionless.

"In that case let's go after the other one and get the body later. No point kicking in doors and getting in a row over the damage. Since he can't move, let's raise the caretaker later and get him to let us in."

I could hear movement, and when I was sure that those who'd been chasing me had left me in temporary peace, I gathered all my strength. Somehow I made my way out of the block of flats and dragged myself down the street by using my hands to pull my wrecked body along some railings. Despite being giddy with pain, I managed to get across the mainline railway tracks, then found a place to hide in a garden. When I saw a man getting into a butcher's van close by I shouted to him, and asked if he'd help me as I'd had a bad fall. He guessed I was an escaped prisoner but I was in luck because it turned out he was an ex-con who was willing to aid me, and became keen to do so when I offered him fifty nicker for his assistance. Together we struggled to get butcher's clothes and a dirty apron over my prison uniform; then I crawled into the back of his vehicle. It would probably have been better if I'd fallen asleep but I couldn't relax sufficiently. We had to get through a police roadblock and their dogs went bloody mad around the van.

"What you got in there?" the old bill asked my driver.

"I'm a butcher, I've got meat in the back."

"Can you open it up?"

"Happily, but only if you'll guarantee your dogs won't become even more crazed than they are now. If they damage my stock then you'll have to pay for it."

"The dogs must be able to smell the blood, I think we'll leave it."

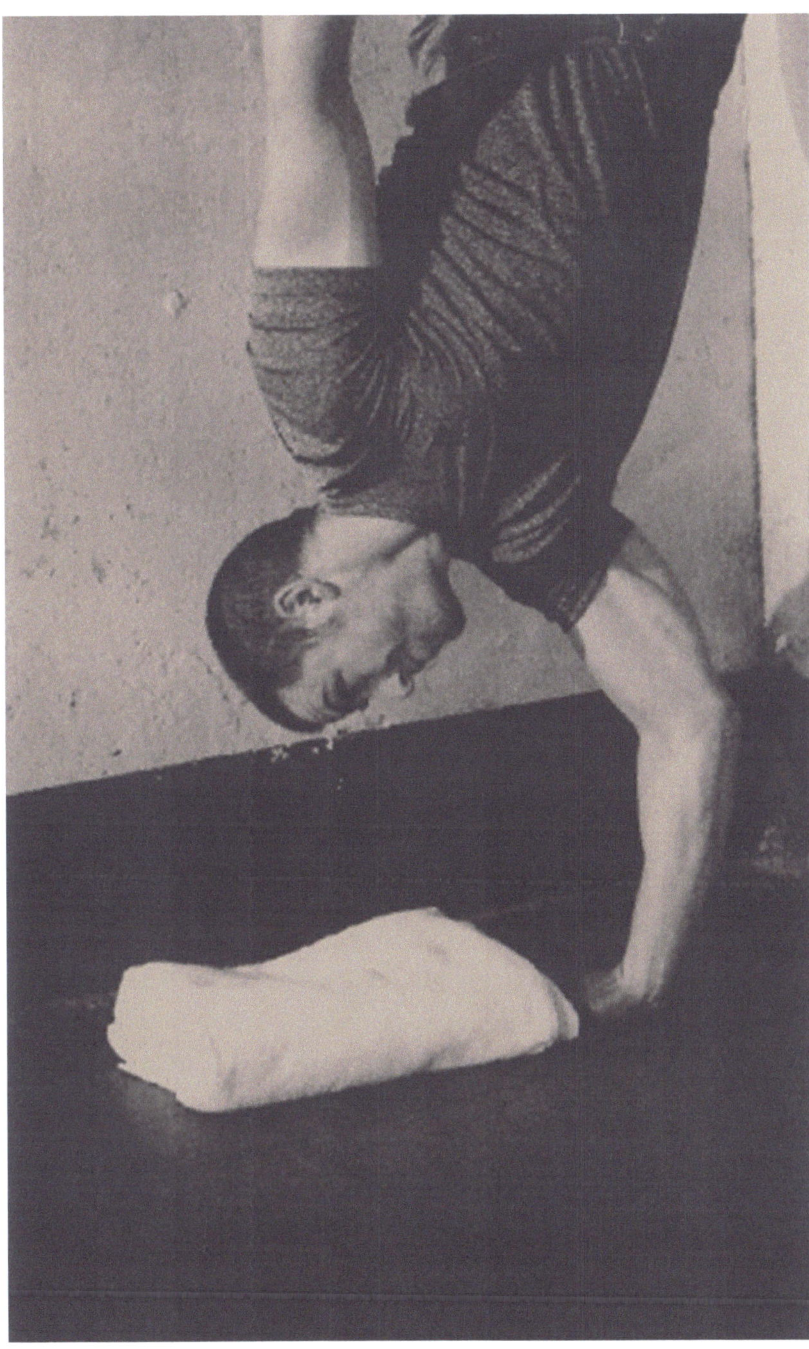

I gave the butcher directions to my cousin's pub in Paddington, told him to go in and tell my relative I'd escaped and that we needed a key for a flat. My saviour came back and drove me around the corner to a room my cousin kept in case of emergencies, but when the landlord saw the state I was in he told us to piss off out of his building. So we went back to the van and I got the ex-con to drive me to my fence Benny Selby's place in Highgate. Once Benny had given the butcher fifty quid and got him out of the door, I told the fence to call my wife Ann, a nurse who worked nights at Queen Elizabeth Hospital in Hackney Road. It turned out she'd already been visited by the cops, and that was how she'd learnt I'd escaped from jail.

When Ann's shift finished she came to see me with a doctor who she knew we could trust. They patched me up, and my wife and her doctor friend saw me through my convalescence, which took months and months. I only stayed a night at Benny Selby's pad; the next day Ann found me a room in Hoxton where I could recuperate. I spent more than two years on the run, during which time I pulled off a series of daring jewel raids –including one against screen legend Sophia Loren when she was filming in England—before finally being recaptured, after a grass gave the fuzz a tip-off as to my whereabouts. Unluckily, Johnny Rider was nicked in Chingford the day after our breakout, so he wasn't over the wall for nearly as long as me.

It is tales like these that made me a legend, but what I want to do is tell you the complete and true story of my life, so you can understand me as an ordinaryworking-class man who acted as he did because of extraordinary circumstances. But rather than start at the beginning, I'll fast forward to where I am now, and then take you back to how it all began.

an excerpt from The 9 Lives of Ray the Cat Jones: A Novel

Marine 1-10

Max Blagg/Alex Katz

A collaboration between Max Blagg and Alex Katz for the *Marine Series'* Exhibition Catalogue, Jablonka Gallery, Berlin, 2008. This piece is an excerpt from the forthcoming book, *Instinct for Bliss: Poems & Prose Collaborations with Artists, 1979-2014*, published by Sensitive Skin Books, late 2015, containing 23 texts by Max Blagg with 23 different artists, including Larry Clark, Richard Prince, Ralph Gibson, Donald Sultan, James Nares and many more

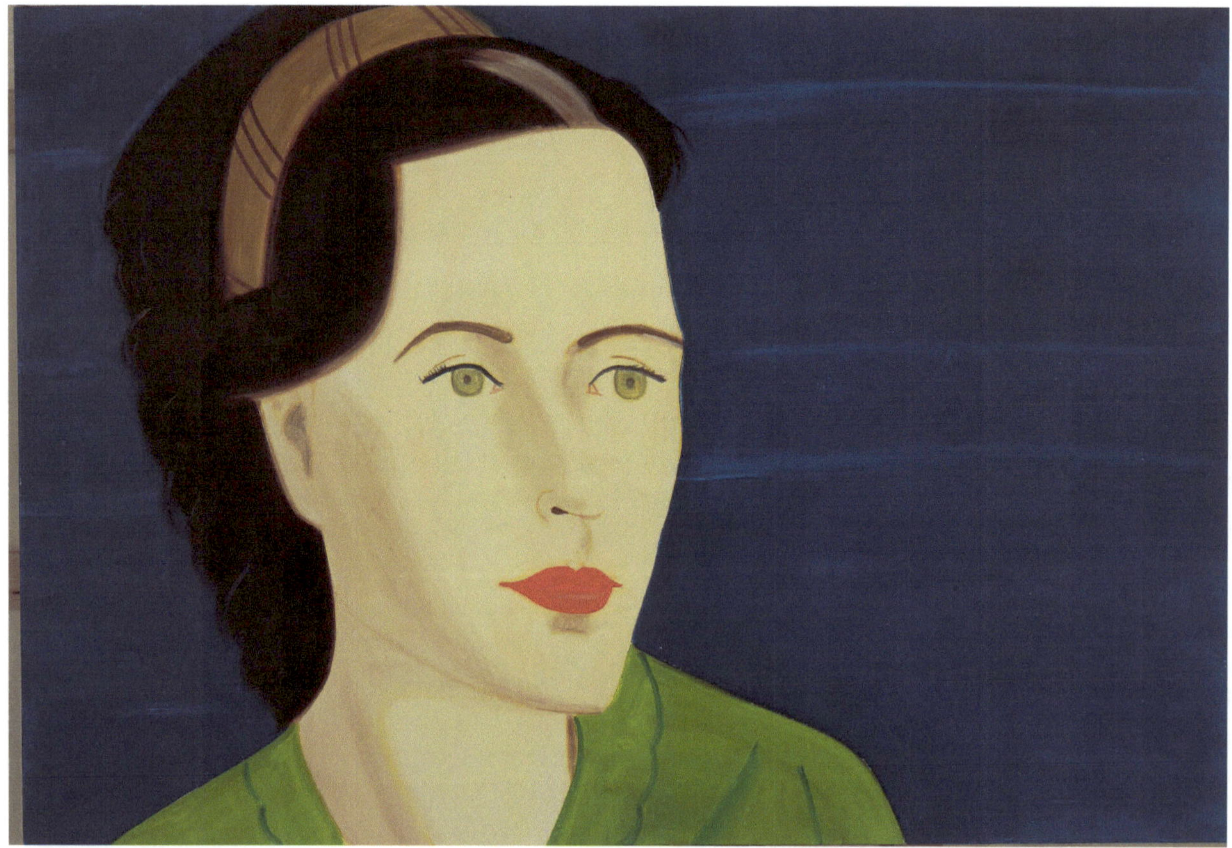

Sharon, 2007, oil on linen, 48" x 72"

1.

A picnic boat glides across the waterway
and when the light hits it turns
into Egyptian gold.
There's beauty everywhere.
I follow it around like a man
chasing pike in a kayak.
August triggers alarums,
paint won't dry electricity shuts down
the sun doesn't move.
Get a jump on the hump of it,
guilt carried off by bicycle to the dump.
Look at the beach
and then look at the beach.

2.

Evening's velvet darkness softening faces and
voices calling from the garden,
blue moon pulling double duty this month
everything stopped spinning and the stars spoke
as clear a language as they speak to sailors
in the wide ocean night;
"sooner or later, one of us must know"

3.

Teetering between the personal and the universe
or simply unnerved by the crazy beauty
of this green world and by what
miracle I remain under it
enveloped in these garlands
of shivery light.
The clouds were pink as nails tonight
the sun went down a fraction sooner
ocean shining like an insect's back
or the black diamond light
of limos waiting outside this week's restaurant.
This is how the dark gets in the door.

4.

New moon slim as a butcher's blade
the Chinese stove housed
the flames of a wood fire,
wisp of apple smoke among the maple,
"go up, little smoke"
make me a place in the pagoda Gautama,
I'll wear my kimono and behave with grace.
August's equatorial heat makes the yeast rise
before the bread, like art before technique
age before beauty sense before rhyme
the branch knocking at the window
in the night a Morse code message
from under the world.

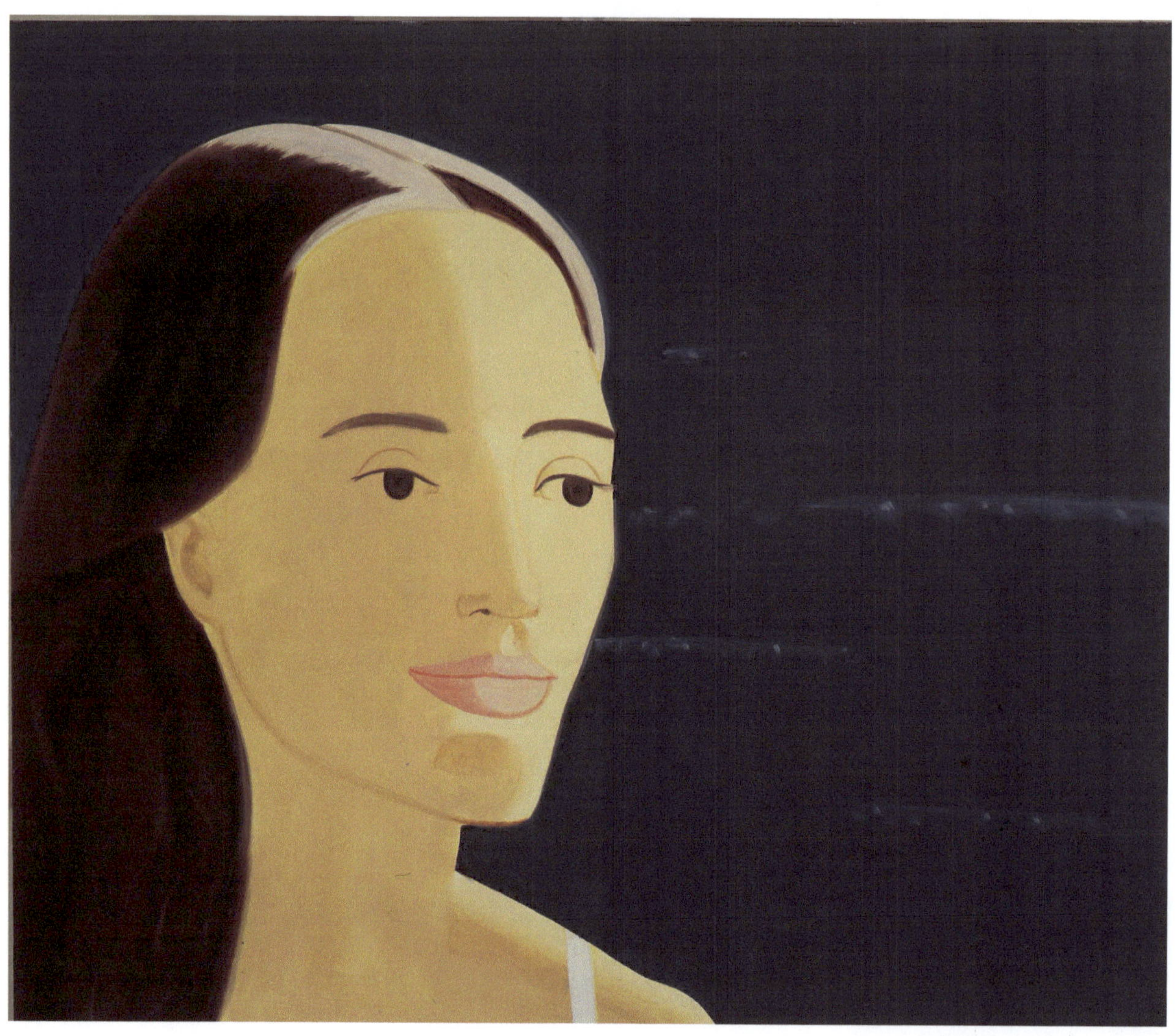

Catherine, 2007, oil on linen 60"x72"

5.

How do you call that part of the body
that recess formed by the collarbone
connecting to the shoulder
that curving little dip of a cup
from which you could sip a tart aperitif?
Or the place where the body
is attached to the thigh
the place where love turns to heat
and flares go up to warn
boaters of turbulence?
"Blue blue windows behind the stars"
lobster boats rounding the point
into open water, eternity blue sky.

6.

Let what remains of this run shaker life
shine clear as a cut stone a spring stream
tumbling downhill to feed the horses
in the long green meadow.
Affirmative says this note from the future
mapped out in the isosceles triangles
incised by age and karma into my palm.
In the parking lot of bright ideas my
spasm key starts you up and the waves wash the
bateau back into the bay where
a cleansing ionic shower explodes above our heads,
bathyspherical slick-coated moutons
colliding in soft skinned air
a semantic loveboat going down
with all hands, shaking our elasticated garments
like the semaphores of an undiscovered race
a trace element of Vikings with black skin and
golden eyes "dark they were and golden-eyed"
I'll take that line and this and this
anything I can conjure here or steal,
the eyes out of your head
or a simple sanctified kiss.

7.

The garden in darkness, no moon,
fireflies signaling from the four quarters
hovering over the damp grass
and my glasses catching a flash
of light sent from the deep blue yonder.
Who calls out my name?
What creatures out there
see me in their dreams?
The silence between tracks
knocks against my ears
grass pressing my face
cool as the cat's fur
coming in from the night
the great joy inside everything
waiting to be tapped out
like sugar from a spoon.

8.

Venus transits the sun but I don't feel her weight.
the morning light is coming toward me,
there are "fields of corn where Troy once stood"
everything bathed in a wave
the gesture of a hand passing over like a shadow
and gone. Grasp that.
The moons of Saturn danced in the telescope's glass
as someone stepped onto the dock
pointing to the sky and the mysteries
contained within it.
The first cup of coffee opens the inner eye
but the second one floods the mechanism.

9.

A summer shower tumbles
like golden coins
into my mouth,
taste the sweetness,
blueberry, violet, aquamarine
tourmaline smooth as
a stone beneath the tongue.
Nerves remain on the inside now,
light pours in from far out in the Atlantic
a righteous light shimmering
like the pearls looped round
your swansong neck.
Some god embedded in it, garden variety
or god of the floating world
shares this sunflower splendor
it pours into the room and you
rush outside into the empty blue air
wishing someone you loved
was waiting there.

10.

Sappho's fragments force-fed into the text
wafers on the tongue, they melted into the
body of work. Stretch that body on this summer
afternoon, leaves already spinning
from the walnut tree,
a hawk drifting at high altitude
as I stand among flowers, eating figs,
black cat nuzzling bare leg.
Life is good, even with your tongue cut out.
Later, under cover of the night
the sky slides down into the sea.

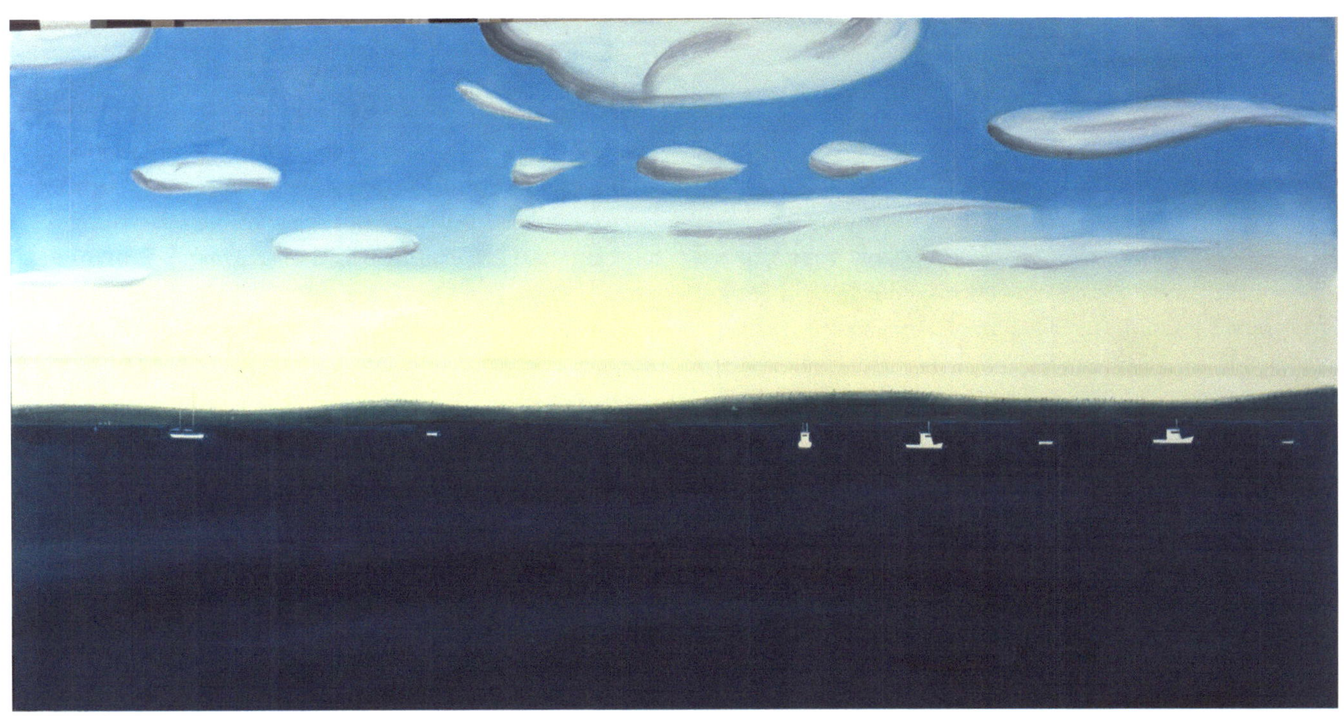

Marine 4.30 pm, 2007, oil on linen 72"x96"

Mugged By A Movie Star

B. Kold

I'M INELIGIBLE TO SERVE ON A JURY. WHENEVER I'm selected for jury duty, I never make it past the first voir dire—the part where the defense and district attorneys interview prospective jurors to ensure they're not biased. Sooner or later, one of the lawyers for one side or another will ask the group, "Have you ever been the victim of a crime?" and I'll raise my hand and tell them, yes, three times. Back in 1986, when New York City was a bit rougher, I was mugged three times within the span of two weeks. Some folks gasp, the opposing lawyers look at each other and shake their heads, and I get to skate.

The first robbery happened while I was at a crackhouse, so I suppose I was asking for it, even though, being a whiteboy, I was looking for powdered cocaine, not rock. And it wasn't even for me. I was hanging out, like I usually did in those days, at Vazacs on 7th Street and Avenue B (aka "the Horseshoe Bar") and I ran into Laura, an old friend I'd last seen when I was living in Paris, (later, ironically enough, she worked on the movie *Traffic*) and she asked if I could get her some blow.

Helpful fellow that I am, I ducked around the corner to the rock house on B and 6th. I went upstairs, checked out their wares and was not impressed—they tried to sell me what looked like Parmesan cheese, really clumpy, yellow crap—so I passed. I went downstairs and while heading to the door at the end of the dimly lit hallway, two gentlemen I'd met upstairs at the crack den—their names, I shit you not, were Sha-hee and Baby Pop—bounded down the stairs, saying "Hold up bro!" and dumbass me, I turned and stopped.

> *He started rolling up my sleeve, like he was a tailor measuring me for a suit, "You ain't got no watch, bro?"*

The tall one shoved me against the wall and stuck the point of a 9" hunting knife up against my throat. I pushed my head back into the wall as hard as I could, to get away from the knife point, which looked and felt very sharp. It seemed like if he gave just a quick little push, *Pop!* I'd be skewered. Sha-hee told me he was mad at me for disrespecting the man's product.

"Should I stick this motherfucker?" he asked Baby Pop.

"Nah, he's all right," Baby Pop said in a friendly tone as he rifled my pockets, transferring my last 20 bucks from my pants to his. The point of Sha-hee's knife dug further into my throat and I started shaking, faking terror.

I don't know why, but I really wasn't scared. I'm not bragging—I'm no tough guy, anything but, I'm kind of a pussy and hate confrontation of any kind, especially of the physical sort, but when I was in the middle of this life-or-death situation, everything felt calm and clear and I was without fear. I remembered a story my Dad once told me about when he was in the war, how he got out of a nasty jam, and I realized I could make it through this safely if I pretended to be scared, so that's what I did. "Yeah, he harmless," the big one said, disgust apparent in his voice as he lowered the big knife. I nodded my head as if to say, yeah, that's right, harmless, don't need that big knife anymore.

Meanwhile, Baby Pop pulled my cigarettes from my breast pocket, peered inside the pack and, finding it empty, shook his head sadly and put it back. Thank you, Jesus, I thought—there were three bags of dope tucked inside the cellophane. He started rolling up my sleeve, like he was a tailor measuring me for a suit. "You ain't got no watch, bro?" I could hear the disappointment in his voice as he found just bare wrist. Sha-hee and Baby Pop turned and walked out the door without even saying goodbye.

When I got back to Vazacs, just around the corner but a world away, Laura was gone. But Evelyn was there, saw the look on my face (now that the moment had passed, I was terrified) and asked me what happened. I told her and she said, "Hey, you can get a free drink out of that!"

She pulled me over to the bar and said to the bartender, "Hey, Mark, give this guy a drink, he just got mugged!"

"Where?" he asked gruffly.

"Two doors down," I said.

He made a face as if to say, "Idiot, got what you deserved." He turned towards a paying customer.

We retreated meekly. Despite her scheming low-rent junky ways, Evelyn meant well and was an all-around good egg.

For the next few days, I saw Sha-hee and Baby Pop wherever I went—not only on the streets of the Lower East Side, but also on the 6 train, Midtown, Wall Street, all over the place—or at least I thought I did.

The second mugging took place a week later, while I was waiting for the elevator in the lobby of my apartment in the Jacob Riis house at 7th and D. (My roommate Tina and I were the only two white folks living on Avenue D between Houston and 14th street in 1986, but that's another story.) I'd just borrowed $20 from somebody at Vazacs for train and lunch fare for the next day, when two teenagers (I don't know how I knew they were teenagers, but they obviously were, even though I couldn't see their faces because they were wearing ski masks) came up from behind, saying "Yo!" I turned around. I think it's safe to assume with a fair bit of certainty that when young men are wearing ski masks, indoors, in May, they are probably up to no good.

"What?" I couldn't believe this was happening again.

"Give us what you got, bitch!" one shouted. They both had their right hands in their bulging sweatshirt pockets, like they were pointing guns at me. Whether it was guns or their fingertips tenting the fabric I couldn't tell.

"Do you have a gun or not," I said. Again, I wasn't being some kind of tough guy. I was tired, wanted to go home and was loaded (I was always at least half in the bag by midnight in those days). After the knife against my throat the previous week, pointed fingers weren't going to get it done. They looked at each other and one of them partially pulled his hand from his shirt and showed me what kind of looked like a gun barrel, but it might have been a stick or even a Tootsie Roll. Close enough.

"OK," I sighed, and reversed my front pockets, showing them white elephant ears. Nothing but lint. I hoped they would be dumb enough to fall for it. They looked at each other again, one of them gestured towards me with his head, the other one approached and dug my wallet out of my back pocket. Shit, thought I was going to get away with it for a second. He pulled the lone, borrowed twenty out of my wallet, and threw the bare billfold against my chest. It fell to the floor while they scampered out the front door.

"Thanks!" I said involuntarily. That made me feel like a chump, but I really was thankful he'd at least given me my wallet back. That was worth a $20 service charge.

But the third mugging was the worst. The third time was a real charmer: I was mugged by a friend, Miguel Piñero, the acclaimed playwright, TV and movie star. He was a Big Deal in the '70s. While he was in prison for armed robbery, when he was 25, he wrote a play, *Short Eyes,* that was nominated for Tony Awards and such. He got out of prison and was embraced by the city's radical elite. He was in movies and had a regular role on (and also wrote for) *Miami Vice.* He was also a convicted felon, a career criminal, a thief, a murderer, and, of course, a notorious junky—the part he played in the classic film *Fort Apache: The Bronx* was not much of a stretch.

I was heading back to my place with Evelyn. It was about 2AM, and it had been a long day, we were both kind of dope sick and we had one mere bag between us. We were just east of B on 6th when I heard somebody shout my name.

"Hey! Yo, B!"

I turned. There was Mikey (that's what everybody called him) across the street, furiously waving his arms over his head. He was wearing a ratty old scarf, a shapeless fedora and greasy fingerless gloves. He needed a shave two weeks ago. By 1986, Mikey's career was on the downside. Not that he cared. He once said to me, while we were wandering the streets late at night looking for a cop spot, "Fuck that Hollywood bullshit, I don't want to sit around Michael Mann's pool, bunch of starlets with they titties hanging out, I'd rather be selling works on Avenue D." The pool sounded pretty good to me, but to each his own.

I stopped. "What's up, Mikey?"

He came trotting over, shambolically approaching me and Evelyn. "You cop yet?"

"Yeah, New York, New York."

"Any good?"

"Don't know, we haven't done it yet."

He pulled a gun, a small revolver, and jammed its blunt snout against my belly. "Give it up!"

"Huh? Mikey, what the . . ."

I really didn't want to give him our dope, not even at gunpoint, not under the present circumstances. It had been a really long day.

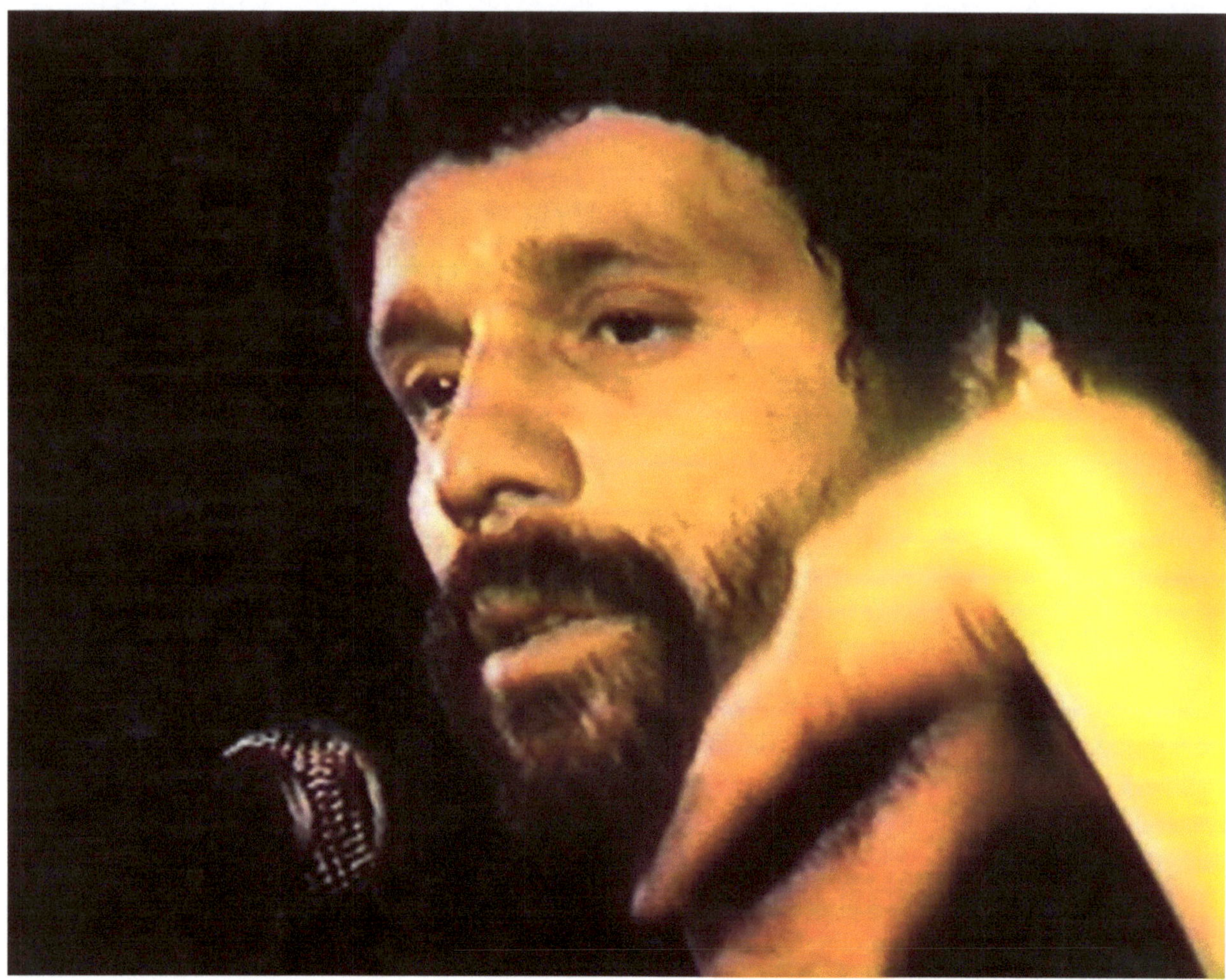

Miguel Piñero reading at the Pyramic Club, 1983. Still image captured from video, courtesy Rick Van Valkenburg

*

It was Saturday. Evelyn came by my apartment in the Jacob Riis House around noon and woke me up. "Wanna go cop?" she asked me.

I was standing at the door in my bathrobe, yawning. "Uh yeah, OK. C'mon in, gimme a minute."

I hadn't been doing dope nearly as long as Evelyn, and didn't have half as bad a habit as she did; I usually waited till the sun went down before I used, I could last till then, and it was generally easier and safer to cop after dark, safer from the cops at least. But I liked Evelyn—she was friendly, cute, tall, thin, high-breasted—and I was glad she'd invited me to participate in her hijinks, so I said "Sure." This is how a man gets in trouble.

Nobody could figure out why Mikey and I were friends. Why was the down and dirtiest, yet most famous celebrity dopefiend on the Lower East Side hanging out with some suburban white boy?

We headed west a couple of blocks and turned right on Avenue B. It was a nice day, early spring, the kind of weather you might get in New York maybe 10 times a year. I liked Avenue B; it had character. Still partially paved in cobblestones, two out of three buildings above 10th Street were vacant shells, so it was peaceful and quiet, a halcyon retreat from the hubbub of the big city. And there were cop spots just about everywhere up there, which made it even easier to relax.

By the time we got up to 13th, Evelyn was pale and sweaty. I was too. Like I said, my habit wasn't nearly what hers was, but the anticipation was making me feel sick, the same way you'd feel "well" as soon as you copped, just from having the bag in your pocket. Liberty was a good afternoon cop spot. We each spent our last ten bucks on a couple of bags rubber-stamped with the Statue of Liberty. You had to hand it to the dope sellers—they had a great sense of irony. Some other brands were Dom Perignon, AA, No Joke, Poison, Toilet and In Too Deep. Couple of years ago there was a big bust in Massachussetts, police confiscated a few hundred bundles of Obamacare. Those dealers could make it big in the straight world doing marketing.

We copped two bags from a spotty Puerto Rican kid, and went back to Evelyn's squat on 8th between B and C. Eighth Street was lined with burnt-out buildings; a gigantic technicolor graffito mural flowed from building to empty building the whole length of the block. It was beautiful.

Her squat was nice and roomy, would have gone for $1500 bucks a month even back then if it was located just a few blocks west (or $15,000 today; or maybe $30,000). It wasn't really even a squat, just an abandoned building "managed" by a crazy old Ukranian lady. Evelyn paid her a shakedown fee of $100 a month to live there. It had electricity from a nearby streetlight via an extension cord, but no running water or heat. I thought it was great, and asked if I could meet the old lady so I could move in. I never did meet her, or move in. The building was converted to luxury condos a couple of years later.

Evelyn asked me, "You mind if I skin pop it?"

"Your house," I said.

I hadn't used a needle yet, though my friends were starting to, so I wasn't shocked or grossed out to see her shoot up. Especially not compared to the first time I saw somebody fix, in the bathroom at Neither/Nor. Neither/Nor was a combination bookstore / performance space / after-hours club / shooting gallery over on 6th Street between C and D. Mikey lived in the back room. Legend had it that on his way to catch a plane to LA to personally deliver his latest *Miami Vice* script, he OD'd on the front steps. When the paramedics arrived, one of them said, "Give him a shot of Narcan." Narcan is the stuff that stops you from overdosing. It also immediately puts you into massive withdrawals. So Mikey, even as he was turning blue, woke from the dead saying "Fuck that shit!"

and jumped in a cab. I don't know if he made his flight or not.

Neither/Nor was a cool joint; they sold underground lit mags like *Between C&D* (remarkable in its time because it was printed on computer paper, with the perforated holes on the sides, and then slipped in a sealed plastic bag), *Raw* and *The East Village Eye.* At night they had poetry readings by folks like Darius James, Emily Carter and The Reverend Pedro Pietri, and music by bands like the Microscopic Sextet, Missing Foundation and White Zombie. I was snorting coke in the bathroom around 4AM with this guy William, who supposedly worked for the film producer Ben Barenholtz, when Sandy, a skanky old junky, started banging on the door. She must have been pushing 40—we were kids back then, and anybody over 30 seemed old, but however old Sandy was, she looked 20 years older.

"Let me in!" she said. We ignored her and kept sniffing. Finally, she pushed the door in, refusing to wait her turn. She sat on the toilet, pulled her pants down, and said, "Don't mind me, I'm gonna shoot this in my pussy." She got out her gear and proceeded to do just that, poking a needle into the dark shadows of her nether regions. My goodness, I thought. I caught a plane to Paris the next day and didn't come back for six months.

She sat on the toilet, pulled her pants down, and said, "Don't mind me, I'm gonna shoot this in my pussy. . . ." My goodness, I thought. I caught a plane to Paris the next day and didn't come back for six months.

Anyway, Evelyn loosened her pants, revealing a couple of inches of smooth peaches. Butt cleavage wasn't something you saw every day back then. Her ass was small but shapely, not quite my callipygian ideal, but I appreciated it nonetheless. She poked a needle one arc radian down along the inviting bright white curvature.

I huffed up my bag with the cocktail straw I always carried. There was no bite to it.

"You feel anything?" she asked.

I shrugged. The dope wasn't completely beat, but it was, as the old-timey New Yorkers used to say, "gahbage." There was just enough whatever the fuck they put in the shit that day to take the sickness off, but not enough to get high.

We decided to head over to Vazacs and cadge some drinks off her ex, a pleasant if taciturn guy who tended bar, while we waited for one of our square acquaintances to show up so we could cop for them. It was Saturday afternoon, there would soon be some yuppie willing to do the old "you buy I fly" routine. Evelyn smiled at her ex and leaned forward, saying, "Hey, can you help us out?" He didn't say anything, just gave us each a shot and a beer. He looked at me and smiled joylessly, as if to say, man, you don't know what you're getting into. Or maybe he just wanted to punch me.

We nursed our drinks while we waited. A lot of dopefiends hate alcohol, but not me. Maybe it was because the "heroin" we were doing didn't have that much heroin in it, was a mélange of Tuinals, Fentanyl, No-Doze, Pixie Sticks and plaster dust, so a shot of whiskey would help get some sort of chemical reaction going. Or maybe I was just an alcoholic before I became a heroin addict.

Bennet walked in. He was a medical student at NYU who liked to hang out at Vazacs on weekends and get high. I always thought of him as a civilian, a guy who'd take a vacation from his life once in a while by spending an occasional night the way we lived every day. Years later I saw him at an NA meeting, making me wrong yet again. He was embarrassed to see me and walked out. I was beyond embarrassment so I stayed. That day all he wanted was a bag, a perfectly reasonable desire, and we were happy to

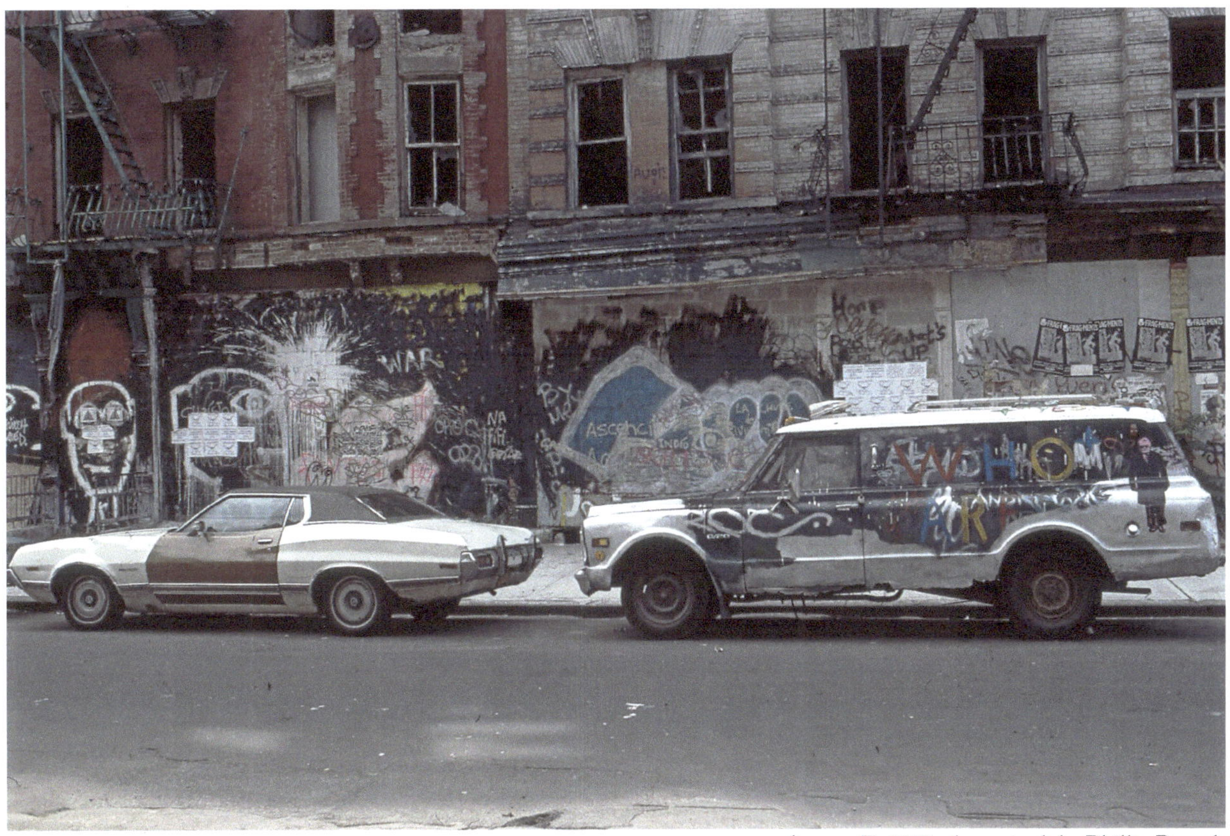

Avenue B, 1983, photograph by Phillip Pocock

oblige, as long as he got us one too. We all grinned as he handed Evelyn 20 bucks.

Why would Bennet pay people like us to buy them dope? There were at least a dozen cop spots within a few blocks of Vazacs, and they were not hard to find. You'd walk down 3rd Street between C and D and there'd be some guy standing on the top of a stoop yelling at the top of his lungs, "Bullet is Opennn! Opennn and Smoking!!! Bulllllit! Bulllllit! Bulllllit!!!" Not exactly on the down-low.

But besides the legit dealers, there were beat artists everywhere, just waiting for a sucker to come along, so they could sell him re-taped dummy bags full of sugar, or rob me, him, or worse. My friend Jack got the shit kicked out of him more than once copping on 3rd Street, but he kept going back there because they had by far the best dope. It was crazy down there, like the Wild West—you'd hear gun shots at least once a week. The first time I copped at Bullet House, with my running buddy Tim, there was a fresh pool of blood on the lobby floor that we had to step over to get to the dealers, who were perched on the stairs. We handed them 20 bucks and one of them asked the other, "Should we take off these white boys?" and the other said, "Nah, ain't worth it for two bags, just serve 'em." So even though they had the best dope I was usually too scared to go over there, unless I went with Mikey—I could go anywhere with Mikey. I'd run into Mikey while I was out copping, and say I was going over to 6th Street and he'd look at me like I was crazy—"Don't waste your money on that garbage, man!"—and he'd take me over to 3rd Street. He'd introduce me to the other junkies and the dealers, saying, "This is B, he's cool," and they'd look at me like they didn't believe him, but they'd leave me alone because Mikey was the unofficial mayor of the Lower East Side.

Nobody could figure out why Mikey and I were friends. Why was the down and dirtiest yet most famous celebrity dopefiend on the Lower East Side hanging out with some suburban white boy? I'm not sure myself. He never hit on me, so it wasn't that. I do remember one time, doing one of the first readings I ever did in public, at Neither/Nor, Mikey was sitting in the back slowly nodding his head. I'd like to think he respected me as an up-and-coming writer. Or maybe he was just nodding out. Everybody found our friendship mysterious, but I guess we just enjoyed each other's company. My less-fucked-up friends were worried about the relationship—did I really need a dyed-in-the-wool junky mentor?

There were easy-to-find cop spots everywhere, but the downside of copping was that you could get robbed before, during or after your purchase, and maybe get raped, stabbed or shot in the process.

And who can forget New York's Finest? By this time, most of my friends had been arrested once or twice. If you got popped and you were unlucky, the cops would beat the shit out of you for fun before hauling you in and then charge you with resisting. Once you got processed and were in real jail instead of one of the big holding pens, it wasn't so bad, not exactly *20,000 Years in Sing-Sing*. Still, spending 48 hours in the system (which felt like a month, especially if you were dope sick), till they finally let you go for time served could be a real problem if you had a job for instance. I usually didn't, but the bologna and egg sandwiches they served for breakfast, lunch and dinner were memorably terrible.

So for a guy like Bennet, who had a real life outside the Lower East, who didn't appear to use more than a bag or two once or twice a week, it was well worth his while to slip somebody like me or Evelyn an extra 10-spot to avoid copping. He knew we knew where the good stuff was (and we did, sometimes) and he wouldn't have to risk getting ripped off or mugged or having to spend the rest of the weekend in a holding cell and miss his Monday morning anatomy class.

Bennet gave us a twenty and we went back up to 13th Street and bought another couple bags of dope, but from a different guy because we were smart and learned from our mistakes. He was standing in the right place, and the stamp looked right, so we thought we were good to go. We got back to Vazacs and Evelyn and I went to the ladies room and split the bag. It barely tasted like anything. Not that good nasty bitter dope taste you learned to love, or even the ether taste of cut-up dope, or even the scotch-tape flavor—this was the sweet taste of crushed Tic-Tacs, or whatever white powder the guy who just beat us put back in some empty bags and re-taped.

Fuck, the fucker burned us! Fucking dummy bags!

But Bennet was cool—he didn't think we burned him. He thought, correctly, that we all got burned together. Not that we wouldn't have burned him if we could have. He gave us another twenty to try again. This time we went to Fourth Street, because at last—it was nice and dark by now—a decent cop spot, New York New York, was open. We delivered a bag to Bennet back at the bar, wished him well and headed back to my place, one bag of almost certainly good dope between us. I was hoping it would be good enough that we could both get high and then Evelyn would sleep with me.

Mikey jammed the snub nose of his gun into my belly. "On three, motherfucker! One! Two!

*

Mikey jammed the snub nose of his gun into my belly. "On three, motherfucker! One! Two!"

I didn't wait for three. I dug the bag out of my pocket and dropped it in Mikey's fingerless gloved hand. He lowered the pistol. "Hey man, sorry about that. I wasn't gonna kill ya. But I would've shot you in the leg if you didn't gimme that bag!" He skulked off into the darkness.

Evelyn looked at me incredulously. "What the fuck! You gave him our dope! What'd you do that for!"

"He was gonna shoot me!"

"Are you sure that was a real gun?"

"Yeah it was a real gun!"

"Aw, man, what're we gonna do now?" Evelyn

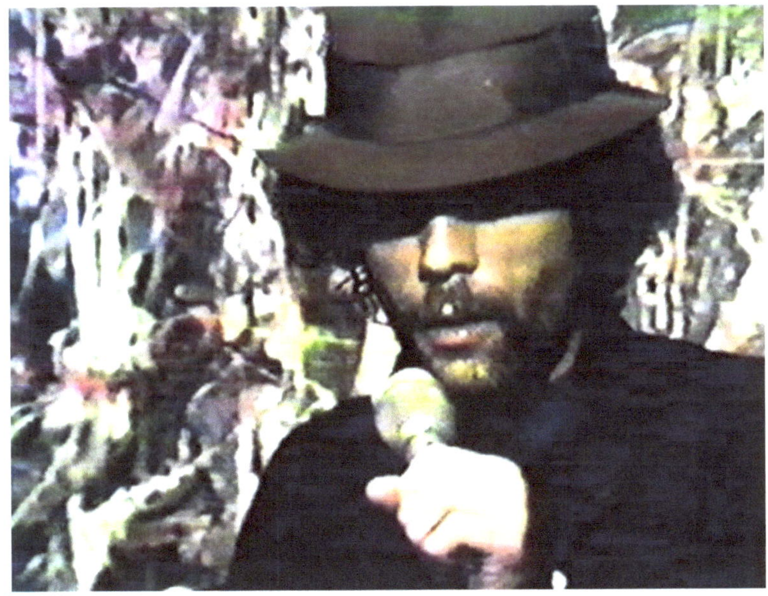

Miguel Piñero reading at Neither/Nor Gallery, circa 1985. Still image captured from video, courtesy Rick Van Valkenburg

pouted. She looked beautiful.

"I've had enough, I'm going home—you wanna come over?"

"You're just gonna go home? You don't want to try something else?" She was appalled by my lack of gumption.

"No, man, I've had it."

"I'm gonna go out there and see if I can cop again."

"Good luck."

I gave her a kiss on the cheek and turned east.

I never did sleep with Evelyn, though I think she wanted to, later, but by that time I was too strung out to care. A few years later I heard she died, of bone cancer of all things. I think she was 32. I wish she'd had a chance to grow up. Maybe she would have gotten clean eventually. Or maybe she'd have ended up like Sandy. No way to tell.

One week later, I was coming home from another shitty temp job, doing data entry at the New York Stock Exchange, just starting to get sick. I was going to go home and change (they made you wear a suit and tie at these temp jobs) before I went out to cop, so I didn't look like a rube. I was walking East on 7th Street, between C and D, almost home, when somebody starts shouting my name.

"Hey B! B-Man, over here!" I turn and look and on the other side of the street, there's Mikey, hopping up and down. Before I can even think about high-tailing it, he starts waving a $10 bill over his head, shouting, "It's cool man, I just wanna pay you back!" He scuttles crabwise across the street and, before I can react, presses a crumpled bill into my hand. What, I wasn't going to take it?

"Man, I'm so sorry about last week, but I was really sick, I couldn't help myself." He whipped off his fedora and tilted his head so I could see his scalp. (I'm not tall, but Mikey was really short, like 5'4" at best; I thought it was really funny that they cast Benjamin Bratt, who's well over six feet, to play him in the sadly mediocre eponymous biopic that came out in 2001.) "I was really fucked up and hurt, too! Check it out, man, somebody tried to shoot me!"

There was a part in his scalp. "See? The bullet grazed my head, they just missed me!" He really said this to me. And expected me to believe him. Like he was Shemp from an old Three Stooges short where they were going hunting and Moe got careless and parted Shemp's hair with a bullet. "I feel real bad about taking you off last week, so I wanted to pay you back. I was glad you just gave me the bag, cause I woulda shot you if you didn't. But I wouldn't have killed you, I'da just shot you in the leg, cause you're a good guy. Anyway, now I'm good—Michael Mann just bought the rights to my life story for $200,000!"

Could've given me $20 then, or maybe even a bundle, to make up for my trouble, I thought, but I didn't say anything.

"So, we cool?"

"Yeah Mikey, we're cool."

I went home, got changed, and copped with Mikey's amend. I don't remember if it was any good or not.

Meet the Beats

Hilary Holladay

WHEN OPPORTUNITY LITERALLY knocked not long after his return from sea, Herbert was ready for a new diversion. It was 1944, the war would soon end, and change was inevitable, even for an unemployed drug addict for whom change usually meant the spare kind he could spend at the Automat. But little did he know, when William S. Burroughs appeared in his Lower Manhattan doorway, that he and his new acquaintance would be forever linked in a literary movement of worldwide impact. The arrival of the future author of *Junky* and *Naked Lunch* would give new direction to Herbert's life, albeit a direction drawing heavily on the criminal life he already knew so well.

That first meeting between Burroughs and Huncke is a signal moment in Beat Movement history. Many chroniclers have described the former as the alienated young scion of an affluent family in St. Louis, Missouri, and the latter as a small-time crook who comically misjudged Burroughs as an undercover police officer—what Huncke called "heat." In broad strokes that is an accurate characterization, but Burroughs and Huncke were not as dissimilar as they have been made out to be. Close in age—Burroughs was a year Huncke's senior—both had grown up at a remove from family prominence, a status that infused their lives with irony and anticlimax. No matter that he would later become a prominent author and celebrity (or that he would kill his wife Joan Burroughs), Bill would always be the grandson of the man who invented the Burroughs adding machine. That was not so bad, especially since it translated into money for Bill. But he was also the son of Mortimer and Laura Burroughs, who seemed to be sliding inexorably down a slope of nostalgia and constrained imagination toward abject ordinariness. That was bad.

Homosexual, possessed of a peculiar wit, repelled by all things banal and bourgeois, Bill cultivated a persona of mordant weirdness. As Neal Cassady wrote in notes about a character clearly based on Burroughs, "By sixteen he was as high-horse as a Governor in the Colonies, as nasty as an old Aunt, and as queer as the day is long." Burroughs accepted his Harvard education and monthly allowance of $150 as his due and let his parents rescue him whenever he got in trouble with the law. Even if he could not bear to emulate their drowsy suburban ways, he was not going to divest himself of material comforts. For his whole life, he had an air of entitlement about him that matched the weirdness drop for drop.

Although Herbert was far from entitled, he recognized Bill's type. He did not have an Ivy League education or a generous allowance to carry him through adulthood, but he had grown up in nice apartments on Chicago's North Side and cherished his memories of elegant luncheons and shopping trips with Grandma Bell, who beguiled him with her tales of life on a sprawling cattle ranch. He knew all about wealth and privilege, which meant so much to his image-conscious parents and the extended Huncke family. But when he began using drugs and spending time with his delinquent pals Johnnie and Donna and the sideshow freak, Elsie John, he was daring the whole Huncke clan to disown him. In seeking out nonconformist, criminally inclined friends who would accept him as he was, he renounced the privileges that came with being a young Huncke in Chicago. To his immense sorrow, his family let him go without a fight. He did not have a safety net to fall back on, as Burroughs did, and the criminal lifestyle he had chosen was now merely his life. When he gazed upon Bill for the first time, he intuitively knew that the stranger before him was exploring one path among a great many while he, Huncke, no longer had any other options.

In retrospect their first meeting at the Henry Street flat seemed inevitable. Bill had come there in search of Huncke's friend and roommate Bob

Brandenburg, who worked at a drugstore Burroughs frequented. In the gun-loving Brandenburg, whom Huncke described as "a friend of mine from Cleveland, a guy like something from a Humphrey Bogart movie, with padded shoulders, a felt hat and a flashy tie," Burroughs saw the criminal connection he needed. Brandenburg, he surmised correctly, would know how to get rid of the stolen gun and contraband supply of morphine Bill had recently acquired from another crooked friend. With Huncke in tow, Brandenburg liked to get high and go to an arcade shooting gallery on Times Square for target practice. It was as close as these two came to enjoying an innocent pastime.

Huncke's first impressions of Burroughs were far more detailed and damning than his often-quoted line about the stranger who looked like "heat." In one of his two published essays about Burroughs, Huncke recalls how Brandenburg presented Burroughs to him and his roommates, Phil White and a man known simply as Bozo. According to Huncke's recollection, Bozo politely offered everyone coffee and tea while Phil made conversation. Meanwhile, Herbert eyed the newcomer: "I had observed Bill only a moment or two but decided I didn't feel friendly toward him—sizing him up in my mind as dull appearing and a bit smug and self-opinionated and certainly not very hip."

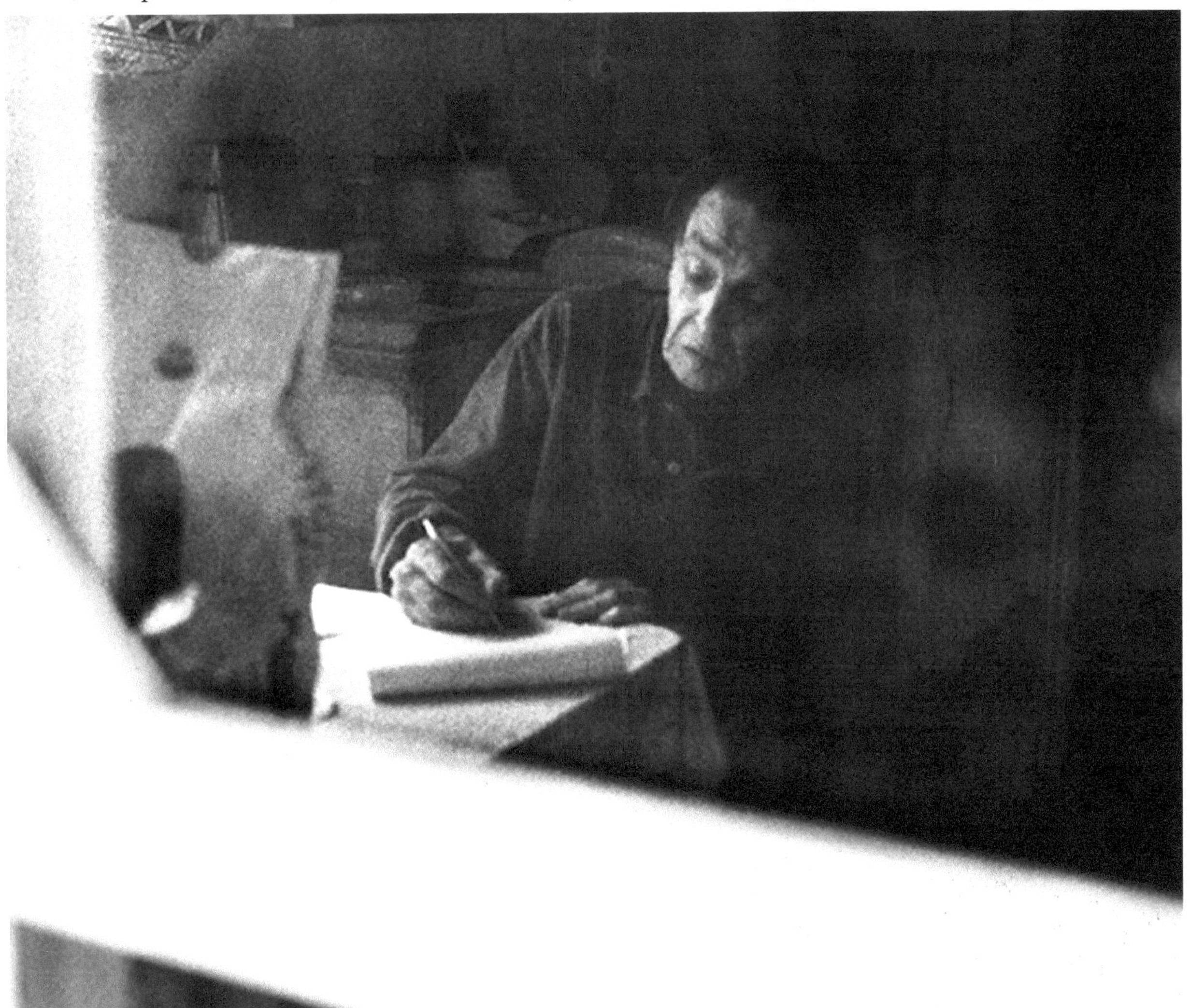

His early antipathy, which Burroughs was quick to pick up on, never quite left him. In recalling his first assessment of the man he would live with in rural Texas two years later, he slips into the present tense, as if Burroughs were standing right before him: "Looking at him intently it entered my mind he could conceivably be a policeman or plainclothesman—maybe even FBI—he looks cold-blooded enough to be one. That old chesterfield coat he's wearing went out of style fifteen years ago, and that snap-brim hat: Don't he think he's the rogue. Those glasses—he looks as conservative as they come in them. Glasses without rims must make him feel like he's not wearing glasses at all. I don't like him—and if Bob doesn't ask him to leave, I will." Without putting his finger on it exactly, Huncke had decided that his new acquaintance was dangerous, and pretentious to boot. There was nothing about the man's appearance that he liked, nothing to inspire trust.

From Bill's point of view, Huncke was a unique specimen to examine and share with fellow collectors of the perverse and bizarre. Herbert realized this and played along for the next fifty years.

But Herbert had a hard time resisting a visitor who came bearing drugs. When Burroughs revealed that he wanted to sell a gross of morphine Syrettes—preloaded syringes of morphine designed for speedy, wartime use—Phil perked up, and Herbert snapped to attention as well. Although Burroughs later claimed he did not have the syringes with him that day, Herbert recalled that all three of them sampled the stash and that, as far as he could tell, Burroughs was shooting up for the first time. "Bill was by this time obviously enjoying himself," he wrote, "and I had to admit to myself just possibly he was a nice person trying to experience something a bit more exciting than what he is usually involved with—and he was apparently honest about his interest in drugs."

From Bill's point of view, Huncke was a unique specimen to examine and share with fellow collectors of the perverse and bizarre. Herbert realized this and played along for the next fifty years. "I believe Bill found me interesting and someone he could use as a sort of showpiece to exhibit before his more conservative associates—as an example of an underworld type—and someone he could rely upon to be amusing and colorful," he wrote. "My storytelling ability had always stood me in good stead, and even then my experience had been varied and considerably out of the ordinary as far as Bill's friends were concerned." His knockabout years traveling around the country, his time in prison, and his adventures at sea provided the basis for fascinating stories, and Huncke himself made a memorable impression, which Burroughs recorded in his first published book in 1953.

In *Junky,* Burroughs describes "the waves of hostility and suspicion" emanating from Herman (the character based on Huncke) "like some sort of television broadcast" the first time they met. "The effect was almost like a physical impact. The man was small and very thin, his neck loose in the collar of his shirt. His complexion faded from brown to a mottled yellow, and pancake makeup had been heavily applied in an attempt to conceal a skin eruption. His mouth was drawn down at the corners in a grimace of petulant annoyance." When Burroughs's autobiographically-based narrator, Bill Lee, presented his business deal to the other two men present, Herman "stuck his head in from the kitchen" and asked one of his friends to join him. Lee heard them quarreling in the other room, and Herman stayed behind when the other man rejoined the group. It was at this point, it seems, that the real-life Huncke warned his friend that Burroughs might be an undercover officer.

With Huncke keeping his distance, it was the violent and volatile Phil White, Herbert's erstwhile sailing companion, to whom Burroughs initially attached himself. The two men became partners in crime picking the pockets of drunks on the subway, buying capsules of heroin when they could afford to, and cadging morphine scripts off disreputable doctors. In *Junky,* Burroughs describes Bill Lee and Roy (based on Phil) targeting an inebriated victim: "We would ride along, each looking out one side of the subway car until one of us spotted a 'flop' sleeping on a bench. Then we would get off the train. I stood in front of the bench with a newspaper and covered Roy while he went through the lush's pockets. Roy would whisper instructions to me—'a little left, too far, a little back, there, hold it there'—and I would move to keep him covered. Often, we were late and the lush would be lying there with his pockets turned inside out." With his illegal activity on the rise, Burroughs had chosen the same path Huncke was on, but he picked Phil White, who would inspire "the Sailor" in *Naked Lunch,* as his criminal mentor.

After White died in prison in 1952, the Beat writers heard that he "was a psychotic killer; fueled by a mixture of Tuinal and heroin, he would get into murderous rages, walking into a store and shooting before anyone had time to sound the alarm." Although Phil's death was written off as a prison suicide, Huncke told friends that Phil had died accidentally in an escape scheme gone horribly awry. In Herbert's recollection, Phil feared retribution from a fellow convict he expected to run into once he was transferred to a different prison. To avoid encountering that man (perhaps someone he had informed on to the police), he planned a fake suicide attempt. His self-endangering act would get him admitted to a hospital. Using bed sheets, he arranged a noose and made it look as if he were in the act of killing himself. The guard who responded to a prisoner's shouts of alarm hit a switch that opened the cell door. When the door swung open, it snagged the rope of bed sheets and fatally tightened the noose around Phil's neck.

Back in the early days of Huncke's contact with Burroughs, when Phil was still alive and on the prowl, Herbert was surprised when the two teamed up. "Somehow there was something ludicrous about a man of Bill's obvious educational background becoming a business partner with knock-around, knock-down, hard-hustling Phil, who had forgotten more about scuffling for money illegally than most people ever learn," Huncke observed. "Still, dope or junk has created many a strange relationship, and this was certainly no more unusual than many I'd run across." When Phil proposed a three-way alliance, Herbert signed on without hesitation.

Burroughs was now spending most of his time with crooks, Herbert prominent among them. The character of Herman is among the most memorable in *Junky:* "I began dropping into the Angle Bar every night and saw quite a bit of Herman. I managed to overcome his original bad impression of me, and soon I was buying his drinks and meals, and he was hitting me for 'smash' (change) at regular intervals. Herman did not have a habit at this time. In fact, he seldom got a habit unless someone else paid for it. But he was always high on something—weed, benzedrine, or knocked out of his mind on 'goof balls.'" By putting street slang in quotation marks, the downwardly mobile Harvard graduate pretended to keep his distance even as he embraced the criminal lifestyle as his own.

Burroughs's cold reportage on the denizens of Times Square stands in stark contrast to Huncke's delicate delineations. The flashes of goodness and vulnerability that Huncke saw in his fellow hustlers, addicts, and thieves either eluded Burroughs or simply didn't interest him. What did interest him was the soul-robbing depravity that went hand in hand with criminal activity. In the same section in which *Junky's* Bill Lee turns his probing gaze on Herman, he describes Herman's friend Whitey (perhaps also based on Phil White), who "combined the sensitivity of a neurotic with a psychopath's readiness for violence." Also at the bar is Frankie Dolan, "an Irish boy with a cast in one eye. He specialized in crummy scores, beating up defenseless drunks, and holding out on his confederates." Then there is Subway Mike, who "had a large, pale face and long teeth. He looked like some specialized kind of underground animal that preys on the animals of the surface." The scene ends with an unprovoked stabbing: "[Whitey] got behind Slim and suddenly pushed his hand against Slim's back. Slim fell forward against the bar, groaning. I saw Whitey walk to the front of the bar and look around. He closed his knife and slipped it into his pocket." Bill Lee never objects to or passes judgment on the acts of violence and cruelty that he frequently witnesses. It seems that he (and by extension Burroughs) is looking to have his faith in man's inhumanity confirmed. With each passing act of depravity, he finds support for a nihilistic supposition: human society is stupid and evil, and defies redemption.

As for Vickie Russell, the friend Herbert writes about movingly in "Detroit Redhead," Burroughs depicts her in *Junky* as a ruthless, possibly deranged creature. The red-haired "Mary" introduces Bill Lee to the dubious pleasures of Benzedrine, a drug extracted from an inhaler tube designed to clear one's nasal passages. The drug-soaked strips of paper encased in the tube could be removed, crumpled into a ball, and swallowed down with a gulp of coffee or some other drink. Bill Lee and Mary spend thirty hours in the Henry Street apartment. Her monologue is memorably debasing: "'If you want to really bring a man down, light a cigarette in the middle of intercourse. Of course, I really don't like men at all sexually. What I really dig is chicks. I get a kick out of taking a proud chick and breaking her spirit, making her see she is just an animal. A chick is never beautiful after she's been broken. Say, this is sort of a fireside kick,' she said, pointing to the radio which was the only light in the room. Her face contorted into an expression of monkey-like rage as she talked about men who accosted her on the street. 'Sonofabitch!' she snarled. 'They can tell when a woman isn't looking for a pickup. I used to cruise around with brass knuckles on under my gloves just waiting for one of those peasants to crack at me.'" This portrait puts a very different face, literally and figuratively, on the vulnerable girl Huncke describes in "Detroit Redhead." Where Huncke glimpsed beauty and frailty, Burroughs mined violence and rage. Although Huncke witnessed, and participated in, many depressing episodes such as those Burroughs recorded in *Junky*, his descriptions make room for an unexpected grace and gentleness. Burroughs's way of presenting criminals in *Junky* confirms our worst fears and elicits an occasional shocked guffaw. Huncke's, in contrast, provokes a much more subtle and empathetic reaction. It is not that he ignores the ruthlessness of his friends and associates. Nor does he neglect his own capacity for being petty, mean, and deceitful. But the depravity that thrilled Burroughs was nothing new to Huncke. It was just one part of a larger human drama—and it was not to be overplayed.

Here, Herbert writes of his life during his drug partnership with Burroughs and Phil White: "My life at the time was in the usual state of chaos with three- or four-day periods of no sleep—making it in a Benzedrine haze—hallucinating—walking along the edge of Central Park peering intently into each clump of bushes, the shadows alive with strange shapes and formations—or of sitting many hours at a stretch in some cafeteria talking with the people of my acquaintance who made up the majority of the Times Square population—a varied and rootless group, frequently homeless and alone, existing from day to day, lonely and oddly frightened, but invariably alert and full of humor and always ready for the big chance—the one break sure to earn them security and realization of the ever-present dream." Few others would have recognized the transient population of Times Square as a community of dreamers, each of whom awaited a big break that would in all likelihood never come. But a sensitive spirit could recognize that yearning in others. Even in a drug-soaked haze, Herbert felt a spiritual kinship with his homeless brethren.

This was the Huncke that captivated Jack Kerouac, who teased symbolic meaning out of his new junkie acquaintance's life just as he did out of Herbert's frequent use of the word "beat." But the future author of *On the Road* did not greatly impress Huncke. When he first glimpsed Kerouac walking with Burroughs in Washington Square Park on a Sunday afternoon, he saw a wide-eyed newcomer rather than a sophisticated young man. In his view, "Kerouac looked like a typical, clean-cut young American college boy. He was as green, obviously, as the day is long. His eyes were flashing around. He was taking in everything and making little comments to Bill, mostly about just the scene in general. You would've thought he was about sixteen or seventeen." Kerouac was actually twenty-three when he met Huncke, but he still clung to the persona of poet-athlete that he had cultivated during his stint as a Columbia football player several years earlier. "I thought of him as a typical Arrow-collar-ad type," Huncke continued.

He didn't try to trade on his association with Kerouac, who would later command the largest following of all the Beat authors. In a 1973 interview, he said, "Kerouac was on the scene, but we weren't nearly as intimate as I was with the others. I saw him but not as often, nor in as friendly circumstances." Asked whether he thought of the young Kerouac as a writer, he replied bluntly, "No, I didn't. It never occurred to me that he would ever write." Although he later seemed pleased that Kerouac based the character of Hassel on him in *On the Road,* it was Kerouac who copied down Huncke's words and called him "the greatest storyteller I know" rather than the other way around.

The day he met Kerouac, as Huncke recalled the occasion, he accompanied Jack and Bill back to Bill's room. Bill had a new drug (possibly peyote, in Herbert's uncertain recollection) he was curious about. "He wanted to find out if it had any kick to it. Would I try it? I thought to myself, 'What have I got to lose?' So I took a skin shot, or a muscular shot, not very large." He experienced no effects, good or bad, but Burroughs was still hoping to get high. Herbert watched closely as he prepared his arm: "Bill had his own way of shooting up, which consisted of him making sure that his sleeve was rolled up as high as he could get it, that there was a bottle of rubbing alcohol nearby, and cotton. He'd dab the cotton into the alcohol and clean off a little spot on his arm, and he'd look at the point on the end of the dropper to make sure that the point was good and sharp. And he'd sort of feel around his arm until he'd located the spot he thought he wanted to use."

For his troubles, Burroughs got a headache. Kerouac wasn't interested in trying the dubious drug. When he and Bill decided to go out for coffee, Huncke declined to join them: "I had a habit at the time and I knew I was just wasting my time talking to them, because I had already sounded them down for money. Bill said he was broke, and Jack didn't have any bread, so I went on about my business. I went back up to the Forty-Second Street area, the area that I knew the best. The area I'd be the most apt to accomplish something for myself in the way of finance."

The encounter was typical of Huncke's contact with the young men who would soon be known as the Beats. In those early days, he saw them as marks rather than friends. They were worth his while only if they had drugs or money to spare, and he was quick to pick up on their mixed signals. On one occasion, fairly early in their acquaintanceship, Jack and Herbert took the subway to Jack's home in Ozone Park. "On the way out we enjoyed ourselves immensely, talking and laughing about things," Huncke recalled. "After we got there and the mother took one look at me, Jack's attitude changed almost immediately." Gabrielle Kerouac didn't want Herbert in the house, and Huncke never forgave her for it: "She dominated [Jack's] life to a terrific extent. She didn't approve of Ginsberg. She didn't approve of anyone that I knew of. I couldn't even tell you what she looked like. She was so evasive and so absorbed in Jack that it was almost impossible to get any kind of picture of her at all. She might as well not have been there, except for the effect she had on him. So I made a long trip back to New York. He stayed on there at the house. He was very apologetic." Incidents of this kind reminded Huncke he was still persona non grata no matter how much he amused his new acquaintances. A novelty, a tattered mascot, he would never be their social or intellectual equal, even though he made a point of reading Dostoyevsky and Jean Genet and other authors his friends admired.

An excerpt from American Hipster: A Life of Herbert Huncke, the Times Square Hustler Who Inspired the Beat Generation, *by Hilary Halladay*

Narcissa

Jonathan Shaw

I was seeing double with fatigue. But Narcisa was just getting started.

She hopped along, from subject to subject, like a cocaine-crazed, hyperactive little fairy, flittering between realms of thought I could barely fathom.

I forced my eyes open. What else could I do? I needed to know all about her paranormal genius mindscape; to understand why Narcisa was the way she was.

As if reading my thoughts, she went on, telling all.

"I no come from de city, Cigano. I know 'bout only de country thing, de plant an' de water an' de weather patterns, an' I know de little animal habitat, an' all they habit. I know where to get de food an' de water an' de real psychedelic mushroom, an' how to make de ayahuasca tea, an' how to talk to de plant e'spirit peoples too. I know all 'bout these kinda thing. But de human e'society, forget it! Is like one big alien program for de Narcisa. *Afffff! 'My e'shoelace, my e'shoes!' Argghhh,* I don' like it de e'shoe an' de clothes, all these e'stupid technological e'sheets, is only for de caution an' de organization! *Fock!* No good for me! What de e'stupid human society wan' for me to do, hein? I don' wan' all de e'stupid peoples asking to me all de day, *'Hey, hey you, Narcisa, what you mean? What do you do? What thing you e'study? Where you work?' Arrggghhh! Shut de fock up! Porra!*"

I stared at her in mute fascination as she powered on.

"Listen, Cigano. When I first come to de city, I go live with de most worse tribe of de *anarcista*. Destruction punks, got it? An' they e'say it all de day, *'Lixo, lixo! Trash trash! Destroy!'* In de city, nothing but noise! *Arggghh!* De whole focking zoological garden can e'scream in their animal language to me now, cuz I don' care! But I am here living in these e'stupid earth, so now I gotta just accept it. What else I can do, hein?"

She stared at me, waiting for an answer.

Bewildered, I shrugged.

Just then, an airplane passed overhead. She ran over and slammed the window shut, holding her fingers to her ears with a pained look.

"Tecnologia! Argggh-hhhh! I got enough of these focking noises an' I don' wan' it no more! If Santos Dumont come up out from de grave today, I gonna take a big e'sheet on his head for all de e'stupid airplane traffic that make me crazy, got it? What de fock I doing here, Cigano, hein? Why I gotta e'stay on these e'stupid planeta? What it can be my mission with de earth peoples? Is no my tribe! No way I ever gonna believe I got de e'same DNA like these focking race of machine builder an' telemarketer! No no no!"

Her voice changed again, into a haunting little robotic drone.

"'Din din! Hello? Good afternoon! May name is Maria, Joanna, Talita, Sofia, Julia, Alessandra, whatever. Din din! We got it de e'special promotion for you, can you buy it? Din din! You got de credit card? I wanna sell to you so I can get more money, so I can buy it on installment plano too. Din din! My name Maria, Talita, Julia, Whatever, bla bla bla . . . ' Fock! E'stupid! Porra! Que merda! Affff . . ."

I watched as she loaded another huge rock into

She hopped along, from subject to subject, like a cocaine-crazed, hyperactive little fairy, flittering between realms of thought I could barely fathom.

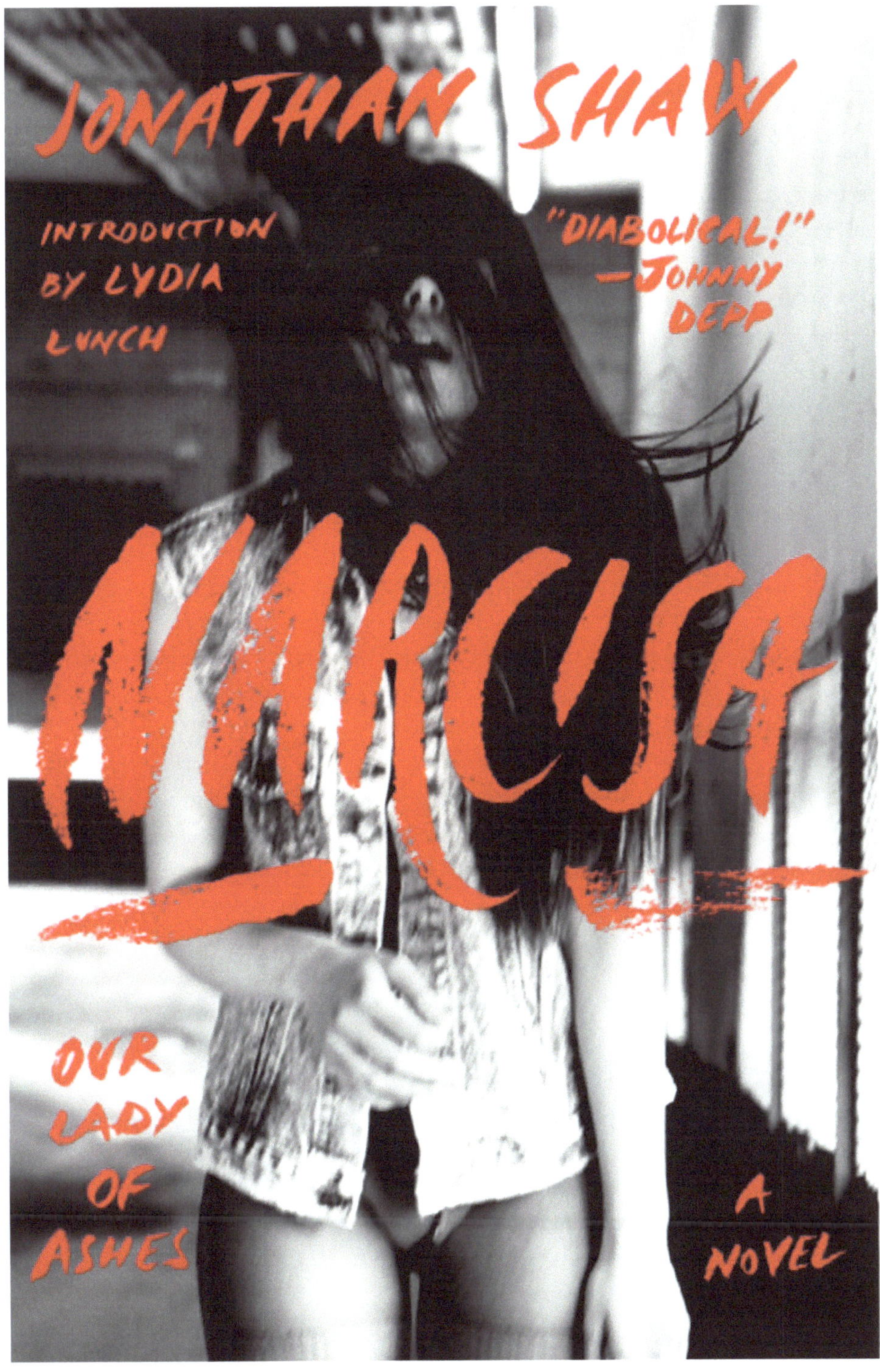

interrupting my drowsy musings. *"Get me de fock out from here, mano! Out!! Arrrggghhh!!"*

I cocked my head like a curious dog as she ranted on.

"All de human systems only exist for disguise it de true nature of de existence! Is only by de anarchy system where peoples ever gonna know themself! De human being is de beast, de killer, de savage, de whoore! I don't even wanna take a e'sheet on you consumer world an' all de human waste production machine! An' I don' wanna make no waste or influence nobody! No focking way! I don' wanna make do nothing on these e'stupid earth! Nada! Porra! Frustration! Arrghh!"

Struggling to follow Narcisa's mad discourse, I felt like I was interviewing an elusive extraterrestrial visitor who was on a tight schedule. Maybe I was. Transfixed, I got out my little notebook and began scribbling away like a nuthouse scribe.

"Arrrggghhh! Din din din din! Hahahaha! Everywhere I go on these e'stupid planeta, de focking earth peoples all de time come an' ask to me e'say all what I know! Arrgh! Fock, Cigano! Why me? I don' wan' it! Don' wan' know 'bout nothing! What I gonna do with so much informations, hein? If I live five

the pipe, fired it up and took a deep, long hit. When she exhaled, there was no smoke.

What th' . . . ? Where'd all that smoke go to? Narcisa! Strange alien physics!

"I don' wanna participate in any of these e'stupid e'sheet, got it?" She sat up, yelping, her eyes blazing,

thousand more year here, I can' e'say all de thing I already know 'bout! Affff! Why?"

I shrugged and kept writing down everything she was saying.

"Is good!" She smiled, gesturing at my note-taking. "Cuz I always gonna be these way, Cigano, you know, so I wan' only for you keep going an' write it down all these e'sheet. I give it all to you, all of who I am, for you to do whatever you wanna do with all these informations. Hah! Maybe *you* can figure these e'sheet out. I only e'say it to you these one thing: Narcisa can be de beginning an' de end of all de thing, de Alpha an' de Omega. But they never gonna put me in de middle of de road here, got it? *Nunca! Ne-ver!"*

Her face seemed bathed in a strange, majestic, angelic glow. "*Porra!* I can think of a million thing to do, mermão. Whatever thing any human being can do, I can do it better. So that's it. *E agora?* What now, hein? What I e'suppose to do? My mind? Hah! Completely without ambition! *Afffff!* Only I wan' exist anymore for teach it all to you now, Cigano, got it?"

I got it. I nodded and kept writing, scribbling, scrambling to get it all down.

" . . . But I don' understand it all de peoples who wanna be de animal doctor, de *veterenario,* Cigano. Why? They wan' be e'specificly doctor to de dog? Or only for horse. For de poodle, or maybe de pony, hein? Or maybe de *pato,* de duck! *Qua qua qua quaaaa! Pato-logia?* Hah!! What about de insect? How come they no got de doctors, Cigano, hein? They got it de cats doctor, de donkey doctor, even de rat doctor, but no got it de insect doctor! Why? *Injusto! Porra! Discrimination! Why, hein? Meow meow! Woof woof! Qua qua quaaa quaaaaa!* An' what about it all these e'specialist doctor? De foots doctor, hein? Do insect got de foots? Wear de little e'shoe? What is it de size, hein? Where do this subject e'start? What it is de relevance, hein? An' then they e'say is me gotta be lock up in de crazy house? Where they get such e'stupid idea, hein?"

I looked up from my writing, holding back laughter.

"I really wan' try an' believe it there some kinda force fields or de metaphysical e'sheets like that, or some very big Somebody who responsible for all these focking question. *Serio!* Is better for me if there gonna be some kinda gods or something, got it? Cuz, fock, mano, what if I gotta be in charge of so much e'sheet only by my self, hein? *Arrrggghhhh! Fock!* Nothing can fill it, de void of de existence, got it?"

I was fading fast, but I got it. Sort of. The bottomless pit ain't got no bottom.

"An' what about these e'stupid e'Stephen Hawking guy, hein?"

"Huh?" I looked up again. The room shifted in and out of focus. My brain was shutting down, melting. Everything was going fuzzy and weird.

"Oí Cigano!" She nudged me on the arm, snapping me back to attention. *"What is it de ambition of all these cripple deficient peoples, hein?"*

I shook my head and shrugged.

"Conspiracy! They wanting to teef it what can' never be teef or be for sale or purchase or find it or give or even inherited, but only can be acquire, Cigano, only by de intellectual naturality of de biological sanity, de e'shielded e'spirit body, use it all they knowledge an' understanding, for go an' destroy ever'thing! Destroy destroy! Why? Argggghhh! E'stupid human race! Clone peoples! E'stupid focking military machine! Heroic champions of destruction! Chaos! Ridiculous competition! Porra! Why, Cigano, hein? Para que?!?"

I shrugged again and again as Narcisa ranted on, her big, mad eyes bulging out of her head like a pair of rocket ships about to shoot off into space.

"Better they got de focking pope in de Holy Vaticano than all these e'stupid politico e'sheets in charge of de earth now! War! Hah! Fock! Was better here when you got it only de priest and sacerdotes to rule you e'stupid planeta! Better I go an' look inside my own focking poosy an' ask inside my asshole, 'Hey, where is de God? Anybody home?'"

That did it.

I began to chuckle out loud. I laughed and laughed, until I was crying; the irrational, cackling, delirious laughter of the insane.

I looked at Narcisa through a haze of humid, sweaty tears. Her face was fading in and out of focus.

Like a ghost.

A Bad Day

Ron Kolm

DUKE KNEW IT WAS GOING TO BE A BAD day, even before he got out of bed. He had a splitting headache, and a lump the size of a nickel bag on the back of his neck. He couldn't remember where he'd been last night—or how he got home. Jill was nowhere around. She'd probably gone out to look for another part-time job.

Duke dragged himself into their tiny kitchen to get a bite to eat. But of course there wasn't a single bit of food in the house—which shouldn't have surprised him—there seldom was.

"Fucking shit," he groaned, "now I'm gonna have to go out."

He took the bike he'd "borrowed" from a friend down six flights of steps to the street. He was sweating and cursing by the time he finally reached the ground floor. Duke aimed himself towards one of the cheap Ukrainian coffee shops in the neighborhood and pedaled off. A bit unsteadily.

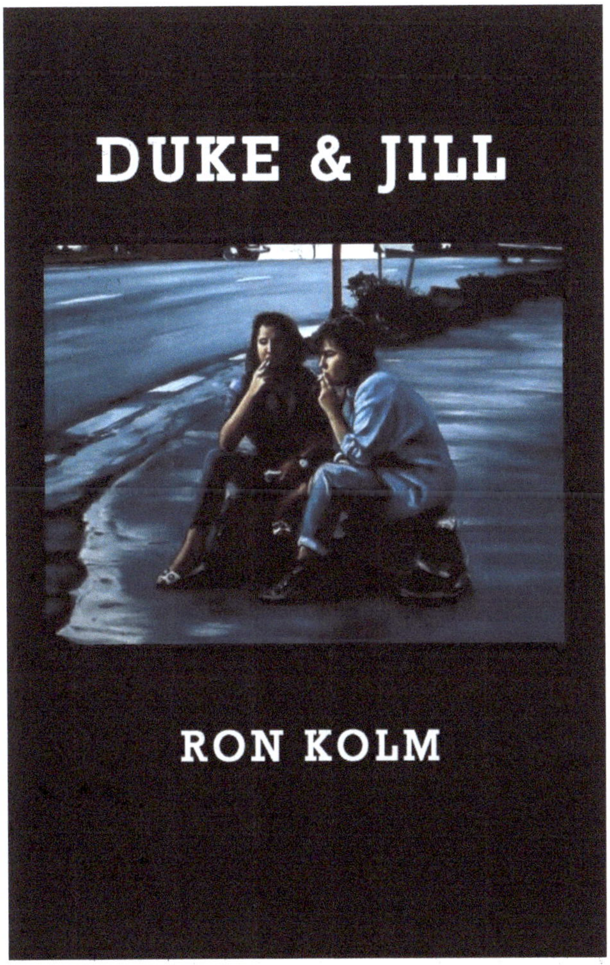

About five blocks from his building he smacked into a pothole. He saw it at the last moment and tried to swerve around it but a speeding *New York Post* delivery truck didn't give him any choice. He broke a couple of spokes and bent the front tire.

"Fucking shit!" he yelled. He righted the bike and started to walk it in the direction of the restaurant.

"Well, my friend," a guy in an army jacket said to him, "looks like you've got problems."

"Yeah," Duke mumbled, noticing that the guy had one hand stuck inside a brown paper bag.

"I'd like to use your wheels for a while," the guy said.

"Go fuck yourself," Duke replied.

"Hey, be cool, man. I got a gun in this here sack," the guy said, grinning. He gave Duke a flash of metal. "And I want your cash, too."

"It's yours," Duke said quickly, letting go of the bike.

The guy took his money and told him to split. Duke went back to his building, his stomach growling. He'd have to get some stuff to sell on the street to get some cash so he could eat. What a lousy day.

But it got worse. He got back just in time to see through a newly smashed door two guys ducking out a window with the few things of any value they had left. Duke was too wasted to give chase.

***

It took him a couple of hours to panhandle enough money to buy a new lock for the door and a sandwich. As he entered his building again a voice called out from behind the stairwell:

"Stick 'em up."

"Fucking *shit!*" Duke said. "I don't *have* anything. We just *got* robbed."

"What's in the bag?" the voice asked.

"A new lock for our apartment and a sandwich," Duke replied.

"That'll do just fine," the voice said. "Hand it over."

"Can I at least keep the *sandwich?*" Duke asked.

"No," the voice answered.

DUKE & JILL

RON KOLM

I'm Starving

Patrick O'Neil

San Francisco, July 21, 1996

IN THE REFRIGERATOR ARE FIVE CAKES: CARROT, lemon, raspberry swirl, three-layer chocolate, and some kind of tiramisu, or maybe it's mocha. I can't tell. Five large, heavily frosted cakes, a slice or two missing from each. Otherwise, the refrigerator is empty. I want a cheeseburger. I want fries. I want anything but cake.

Two days ago Saul and I robbed a local bakery. Saul took the cakes too. Hungry, I stand in front of the refrigerator with the door open. At my feet is a cat. I stare at the cat. It stares at me. I look at the cakes. So does the cat. I look back at the cat. It looks up at me.

"Hey, whose fuckin' cat is this?" I ask. The kitchen window is open. I push the cat toward it with my foot. The cat looks at me, looks at the cakes, and walks toward the window, its tail sticking straight up in the air.

"It's a fuckin' zoo," I say. "It's a fuckin' cat zoo with cakes."

"Who are you talking to?" Jenny's in the bedroom, in bed. We've done our morning shots. I'm in that space where I know I have to figure out what I'm doing today. I have to eat. I have to get Jenny to eat. I have to do a robbery. I have to score more drugs. I have to buy cigarettes. I have to put some clothes on. I'm standing in front of the refrigerator, naked.

"There's some strange cat in here."

"A Siamese?"

"Yeah."

"That's our cat."

I push my finger into the thick white icing on the carrot cake, scrape off an inch and stick it in my mouth. The combination of butter, cream cheese and sugar explodes on my tongue and I almost gag. I close the refrigerator, pick a half smoked cigarette from the ashtray, lean down, and light it off the stove.

"We got a fuckin' cat?"

Saul is in the bathroom standing in front of the mirrored medicine cabinet. He's applying theatrical glue to his face. With a practiced movement, he presses the fake beard and mustache to his upper lip and chin. He turns, sees me watching standing in the doorway. He looks like some demented lumberjack-junkie, except he's dressed in a three-piece suit. I'm dressed in slacks and a button down shirt. I can't find my shoes.

"Jenny, you seen my shoes?"

She doesn't answer. She's probably asleep. Jenny can sleep. Like all day long. I dig through a pile of dirty clothes, find a wrinkled tie and put it on. The toe of one of my shoes sticks out from under a chair. I reach down, grab it, see the other one, and pull it toward me.

Saul is waiting by the door, attaché case in hand. I pick up my suit jacket and we walk out into the alleyway that leads to the front of the building.

"You got the piece?" I ask. Saul pats the inside breast pocket of his suit and smiles. I light a cigarette as we walk toward the supermarket two blocks away. It's a beautiful afternoon. The sun is shining, the sky is clear. My mouth tastes like shit. I forgot to brush my teeth.

"Is my breath bad?" I say and lean towards Saul and blow at him.

"Don't breathe on me," says Saul. His newly acquired facial hair looks really fake in the sunlight.

In the supermarket parking lot I spot what we need: It's an older Honda Civic that looks to be in good shape. I slip the slim jim's hooked end down between the window and the door's rubber seal and jiggle it until it catches, then abruptly pull it upwards. The door's lock mechanism clicks. I open the door and get in.

I take a screwdriver and wire cutters from my suit pocket and force the plastic housing off the steering column and then jam the end of the screwdriver into the ignition. Prying the entire lock off I expose the three contact points attached to the wires: power, ignition, and starter. With the cutters I snip the wires, then strip the ends and twist the power and ignition together, and touch the starter lead, which sparks as I press the gas pedal. The engine hesitates then roars to life and I feel smugly satisfied at having picked the right car.

I lean over and unlock the passenger door and Saul gets in. I hit the gas and pull out of the parking lot as I light another cigarette and adjust the rearview mirror. I look at Saul. He looks tense. The bank is only five minutes away.

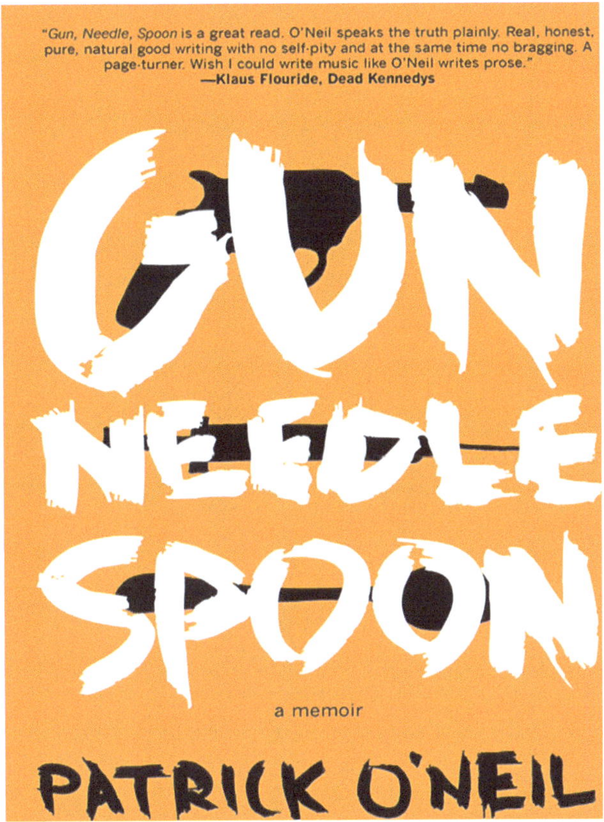

"Why do I have to go in alone?" says Saul.

"We've been over this," I say. Saul can't drive. He never learned how. "Can't leave a stolen car running at the curb. It just doesn't look right. It says, hey, there's a fuckin' robbery going on. I know how to drive. I stay with the car."

"I hate going in alone."

It is always better to have two people for a bank job. It can get a little crazy inside. We've looked around, but everyone we know who dabbles in this sort of activity is either too high, too sketchy, or just way too insane. The last thing we need is someone's nerve getting the better of them. Then there we are coming out of the bank and the car is gone. Not my idea of a getaway.

Turning onto Union Street I drive past the bank. There's no one out front, and the pedestrian traffic on the sidewalk is relatively sparse. A mailman with a large leather bag slung over his shoulder chats with a woman standing in the doorway of a high-end boutique.

"Drive 'round the block," Saul says. A precaution we always take. Never know if a cop is eating at a local restaurant, or some meter maid with a police radio is close by handing out parking tickets.

The neighborhood is quiet. Everything seems normal. I pull up to the bank's front door and double-park. Saul sighs, gets out and walks into the bank. I adjust my tie in the rearview mirror. Traffic is light. There are no cars behind me. I look over at the bank, but can't see in the window, the sun's reflection is too bright. Down the block an oncoming car stops and backs into a parking space. I look in the rear-view mirror. I look over at the sidewalk. I glance at the bank. Sweat runs down my facc. A city bus passes. A woman pushing a stroller stops in front of a store and then continues walking. I look at the gas gauge. The tank is half full. I want a cigarette, but I don't want to lose my concentration. I check the rearview mirror. See my reflection. I glance at the bank. I look across the street. A woman gets out of her car, walks around to the parking meter. I check the rearview mirror again. I wipe my forehead with my hand and run my fingers through my hair. Then reach over and open the passenger door. I look over my shoulder. I look at the bank. I release the parking brake. I grip the steering wheel and look over as Saul comes out and walks to the car.

Before he's all the way inside I push down hard on the gas pedal and we take off, tires squealing. My heart pounds as the car accelerates. At high speed I make the intersection, swerve around the corner, drive two blocks, and turn again. Sliding through the next intersection. I ignore the stop sign, slip in between a taxi and a delivery van, then make a quick left and drive down a deserted alley.

Saul opens the attaché case; inside are two stacks of twenties, a few loose hundreds, tens and fives. It's an okay haul. You never get as much as what you're expecting. Thumbing through a wad of money Saul stops when he feels a strange piece of plastic.

"Look at this," he says and holds up a clear circuit board with metallic copper strips and a small round battery glued to the back of a twenty.

"Tracer?" I say.

"Who the fuck knows? It sure as hell ain't money," he says and hands it to me with a couple of loose bills—getaway money once I ditch the car.

Two blocks before my apartment building, I slow down. At the corner I pull to the curb and Saul gets out, casually adjusts his suit, and walks away, briefcase in hand. I push down hard on the gas, drive to the end of Fillmore Street and maneuver the car into the commuter traffic on Marina Boulevard. Five minutes later I make a right at the entrance to the yacht club and slip into the first open spot in their parking lot. Picking up my tools I place them in my coat pocket and get out, kicking the door closed with my foot.

The Golden Gate Bridge rises in front of me out of the Bay, the water glistening in the afternoon sun—a nice view any other time. I walk past the sailboats moored at the dock, stop at a trashcan and toss in the weird circuit board. At a concession stand I buy a pack of cigarettes, take one out, light it, and walk along the breakwater toward home.

Bank jobs are a motherfucker. Even when I'm driving my adrenaline's pumped so high I'm jacked up for hours afterwards. Going inside is even worse. Your senses are so hyped up. There's all these people staring at you, scared as hell—you definitely have to have your intimidating demeanor down to a science to be in control. It's all in the acting, baby.

The minute you pull the gun you have ninety seconds to finish the job and get out. As ninety seconds is the minimum possible amount of time it takes the police to respond to a bank's silent alarm. If you're alone, you stand in line waiting your turn and when you get to the teller you show the gun. You have to be discreet. You have to act quickly. You have to get in and get out before somebody realizes what's going on and triggers the alarm.

Below the counter is the working cash drawer, which holds a few thousand dollars and is the quickest to access. The other, the large drawer, holds more, but takes an additional key to open, which takes more time. Unless you're doing a takeover job where one gunman holds everyone at bay while another empties the drawers, your best chance is the working drawer and whatever money is inside.

Then there are the disguises: glasses, fake beards, mustaches, even fake ponytails hanging out the back of baseball caps. Cheap suits, athletic gear, army fatigues, and security guard uniforms can be worn over regular clothing and then tossed—anything to confuse witnesses. We once went in wearing motorcycle helmets and riding gear then fled the scene in a van certain the cops were on the lookout for anyone on a bike that fit our description. Stolen cars, taxicabs, and bicycles all come in handy for getting away. Although I've simply just walked off, blending into the crowd.

When I cross Marina Boulevard I see the dope man's cheesy Mustang in the driveway of my apartment building. Jenny must have called him the minute Saul walked in the door.

* * *

The dope is strong. My eyes barely open as I pull the rig out of my arm. I scratch the bridge of my nose and fumble with the cigarettes, but I can't seem to get hold of one. Dropping the pack I lie back and feel warm dullness through my entire body. I remember thinking something about my mother, but can't remember what it was. I stare at the television. A masked boogeyman runs a butcher knife across a woman's throat, the sound turned so low her screams are far away. The cat jumps up, walks across the bed, and stands on my chest. Its paws feel like steel rods pressing into me, its face inches from mine.

"Whose fuckin' cat is this?" I ask and then pet it on the head and scratch behind its ears—the purring becoming louder as I close my eyes.

An excerpt from GUN NEEDLE SPOON, *published by Dzanc Books, 2015.*

Contributors

Jacques Mesrine (28 December 1936–2 November 1979) was a French criminal. He was responsible for numerous murders, bank robberies, burglaries, and kidnappings in France and Canada. Mesrine repeatedly escaped from prison and made international headlines during a final period as a fugitive when his exploits included trying to kidnap the judge who had previously sentenced him. An aptitude for disguise earned him the moniker "The Man of a Thousand Faces" and enabled him to remain at large while receiving massive publicity as a wanted man. Mesrine was widely seen as an anti-establishment "Robin Hood" figure.

Catherine Texier is the author of four novels, *Chloé l'Atlantique, Panic Blood, Love Me Tender* and *Victorine,* and the memoir, *Breakup,* which was featured on Oprah. She was coeditor of the groundbreaking literary magazine, *Between C and D,* and is the recipient of a National Endowment for the Arts Award and two New York Foundation for the Arts Fellowships. Her latest novel, *Victorine,* won *ELLE Magazine's* 2004 Readers' Prize for Fiction. Her short stories, essays, and reviews have appeared in such places as *The New York Times, Newsday, Harper's Bazaar,* and *Cosmopolitan.* She lives in New York City.

Justin Clifford Rhody is a photographer based in Oakland, California. His work has been exhibited extensively in galleries, traveling slideshows, photo blogs and a self-published zine titled *Slo-Mo.* His first photobook, *Sliding Glass Door,* was published in 2012. A monograph of photographs shot in Central America 2009-2012 titled *Zona Urbana* was published in the spring of 2015 by Mirro Editions. Rhody is also the curator and host of Vernacular Visions, a public slideshow series of found 35mm slides. For more information, visit www.justincliffordrhody.com.

Peter Blauner began his career as an assistant to journalist Pete Hamill and spent the 1980s covering crime, politics and other forms of socially-abhorrent behavior for *New York* magazine. His six novels include *Slow Motion Riot* (winner of an Edgar Allan Poe award for best first novel) and *The Intruder,* a *New York Times* bestseller. He has written for several television shows in the *Law & Order* franchise as well as *Blue Bloods.* His short fiction has appeared in *Best American Mystery Stories* and on NPR's *Selected Shorts from Symphony Space.* His work has been translated into twenty languages, most of them understood by other people.

Hal Sirowitz is a frequent contributor to *Hanging Loose Magazine, The Bellevue Literary Review, Manhattan Review* and the *Assinine Review.* He was the winner of The Nebraska Book Award 2013 Poetry Book Competition for his last book, *Stray Cat Blues.* He has been published in *The Southampton Review, Failbetter* and *The Los Angeles Jewish Forward.* He lives in Philadelphia, Pennsylvania.

Thaddeus Rutkowski is the author of the books *Violent Outbursts, Haywire, Tetched* and *Roughhouse. Haywire* won the Members' Choice Award, given by the Asian American Writers Workshop. He teaches at Medgar Evers College and the Writer's Voice of the West Side YMCA in New York. He received a fiction fellowship from the New York Foundation for the Arts. He lives with his wife and daughter in Manhattan and recently performed in the City Slam in Dublin.

Robert C. Hardin's short-story collection *Distorture* won the Firecracker Award and was nominated for a Bram Stoker. His fiction and short stories have languished in the anthologies *Avant-Pop: Fiction for a Daydream Nation, Postmodern Culture,Storming the Reality Studio, In the Slipstream, Forbidden Acts,*

Mississippi Review's Best of the Web Anthology, Storming the Reality Studio: A Casebook of Cyberpunk & Postmodern Science Fiction, and *An Exaltation of Forms.* As Hardin frequently complains while scuttling from bar to bar and wearing children's clothes, his work has also faded unacknowledged in back issues of the *Evergreen Review, Postmodern Culture* (Oxford University Press), *Fiction International, Mississippi Review, New York Press* and *Funeral Party.* As a studio musician, he has piddled away invisibly on more than thirty albums.

Julia Kissina is a photographer and writer born in Kiev, Ukraine. She graduated from the Academy of Arts in Munich in 1998 and now lives in Berlin. Her work has been exhibited extensively throughout Russia, Germany, France and Italy. Her best-known books include *Dead Artists Society* and *When Shadows Cast People.* Her work has appeared in *Harper's* magazine. For more information, visit www.juliakissina.de

A recipient of an NEA fellowship in poetry and an Edgar Award in fiction, **D. James Smith's** poems and stories have appeared recently in *The Malahat Review, New Millennium Writings* and *The Notre Dame Review.* His books include two collections of poems, *Sounds The Living Make* (S. F. Austin State Univ., 2012), *The Dead Ventriloquist,*(Ahsahta,1995) and the novel, *My Brother's Passion* (Permanent Press, 2004) as well as four novels in children's literature.

Christopher Romero studied Poetics at New College of California with Robert Duncan and others. He plays Balinese Gamelan with Dharma Swara in NYC and has performed at the Bali Arts Festival, Symphony Space, the U.N. and The Stone. As a solo artist, he has created two albums of material, *Pretty Sketchy* and *Some Are.* He is currently working on a book of songs.

Carl Watson is a poet and fiction writer who splits his time between NYC and a barn in the Catskill Mountains. His most recent book of poems is *Astral Botanica* (Fly By Night Press / Gathering of the Tribes, 2014). Other publications include: *Backwards the Drowned Go Dreaming, A Novel* (Sensitive Skin Press 2012); *The Hotel of Irrevocable Acts, A Novel* (Autonomedia / Unbearables Press, 2008) and the short-story collection *Beneath the Empire of the Birds* (Apathy Press, 1997). Watson has been a regular columnist for *The Williamsburg Observer* and *The Ninth Threshold,* along with other online and print journals. He is the recipient of the Kathy Acker Award for Fiction in 2012.

Stewart Home is the author of more than a dozen published novels and several books of cultural commentary. He has also worked in the visual arts since the 1980s. He has an upcoming solo show at Queens Park Railway Club titled *The Tarot of Bruce Lee,* which will be part of the Glasgow International Festival in 2016.

Max Blagg was born in England and has lived in New York City since 1971. He is the author of four collections of poetry and several other books. He has collaborated with various artists, including Jerelyn Hanrahan, Jack Pierson, Richard Prince, Keith Sonnier and Larry Clark. He is editor-at-large for *Man of the World Magazine,* contributing editor to *Oyster Magazine* and *10 Magazine,* and a member of the Photography Faculty at the School of Visual Arts / NYC. A new collection of writings, ***Slow Dazzle,*** is forthcoming from Sensitive Skin Press.

Alex Katz was born in Brooklyn, New York in 1927 and studied at the Cooper Union. His work has been shown in more than 200 solo exhibitions internationally since 1951, including the Whitney Museum of American Art, the Brooklyn Museum and the Jewish Museum in New York; the Irish Museum of Modern Art in Dublin; and the Saatchi Gallery in London. His work is featured in the collections of over 100 public institutions worldwide, including the Museum of Modern Art and the Metropolitan

Museum of Art in New York; the Smithsonian Institution in Washington, D.C.; the Carnegie Museum of Art; the Art Institute of Chicago; the Tate Gallery in London; the Centre Georges Pompidou in Paris; Museo Nacional Centro de Arte Reina Sofia in Madrid; the Metropolitan Museum of Art in Tokyo; and the Nationalgalerie in Berlin.

Outsider artist **Samoa Moriki** was born in a sleepy fishing town in Hiroshima, Japan. He moved to New York City in 1980 and became a major figure in the Lower East Side art scene. He is the co-founder and guitarist of the legendary shock-rock performance art rock band, The Voluptuous Horror of Karen Black.

Matt McLaren lives in Hollywood, California and has previously written for film, TV and stage. His stories can be found in *The Cortland Review* and *Embodied Effigies*.

David de Biasio is an Italian painter originally from Venice, Italy. His work has been exhibited in London, Paris, New York, Toronto, California and throughout Italy.

Originally from Los Angeles, **Erik Noonan** is the author of the poetry collections *Stances* and *Haiku d'Etat*. His writing appears in *The Denver Quarterly, The Invisible Bear, 32 Poems Magazine, Forum, Samizdat, SubtleTea,* and *Cross-Strokes: an Anthology of California Poetry*. Noonan lives with his family in San Francisco.

Jonathan Shaw, the son of jazz legend Artie Shaw and the glamorous Hollywood starlet Doris Dowling, is a world-traveling outlaw artist, gonzo journalist, novelist, blogger, spoken-word performer, witch doctor, anti-folk hero and underground philosopher. He resides in Rio de Janeiro, but makes frequent visits to other home bases in New York City and Hollywood.

Hilary Holladay is a scholar of American literature who lives in Charlottesville, Va., and teaches at James Madison University in nearby Harrisonburg. Her writing focuses on the Beat Movement and modern and contemporary African American literature. She is the former director of the Kerouac Center for American Studies at the University of Massachusetts in Lowell, Jack Kerouac's hometown.

Ron Kolm is one of the founding members of the Unbearables literary collective, and an editor of several of their anthologies: *Crimes of the Beats, The Worst Book I Ever Read* and *The Unbearables Big Book of Sex!* He is an associate editor of the *Evergreen Review*. He is the author of *The Plastic Factory* and the co-author, with Jim Feast, of the novel, *Neo Phobe*. A collection of his poems, *Divine Comedy*, has just been published by Fly By Night Press. He's had work published in *Live Mag!, Gathering of the Tribes* and *The Outlaw Bible of American Poetry*. Kolm's papers were purchased by the New York University library, where they've been catalogued in the Fales Collection as part of the Downtown Writers Group.

B.Kold was one of the original founders of the precursor to *Sensitive Skin,* the 1990s Lower East Side literary journal *Peau Sensible*. He currently lives in a yurt in the Lolo National Forrest in Montana.

Patrick O'Neil is a former junkie bank robber and the author of the memoir *Gun Needle Spoon* (Dzanc Books). His writing has appeared in numerous literary and pop culture publications, he has been nominated twice for Best of the Net, and is a regular contributor to the recovery website *AfterPartyMagazine*. O'Neil holds an MFA in Creative Writing from Antioch University Los Angeles, and teaches at AULA's inspiration2publication program, and Los Angeles Valley College. O'Neil recently relocated from the glittery sleaze of Hollywood to live in LA's monument to broken dreams, the über hip Downtown district with his girlfriend and two giant Maine Coons. For more information please go to: www.patrick-oneil.com

Sensitive Skin Books

on sale now at Amazon.com and select bookstores!

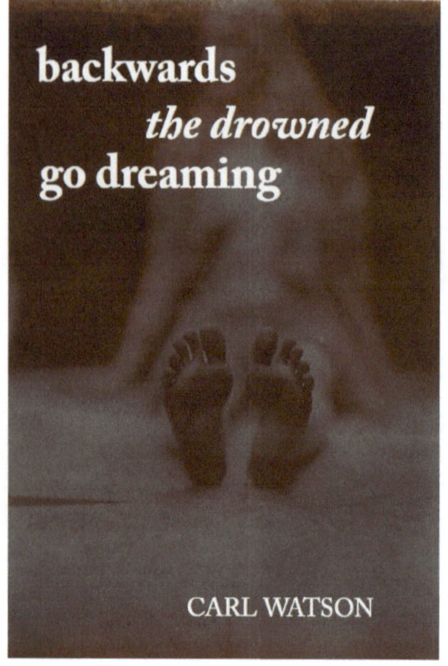

"[Watson] writes like someone who pushed himself to the wall, then pushed through it to the void and came back with stories to tell. Here he reclaims the Seventies, one of the more desolate of recent epochs, with the clarity of Proust, the balefulness of Bodenheim, and the raw honesty of an Iggy song."

—John Strausbaugh, author of *Black Like You* and *Sissy Nation*

"With prose unfurling like cigarette smoke bleeding into that cloud of half-forgotten memories forever shadowing missed opportunities that hangs over a noonday dive somewhere during the twilight of the last blown century, heartbreak rock-n-roll on the radio crackling in exquisite precision between AM stations and windswept interstates, Carl Watson daydreams before silent black-and-white televisions in SRO lobbies or as he drinks himself sober in crumbling Chicago tenements. *Backwards the Drowned Go Dreaming* explodes the bleary-eyed myth of the American road."

—Donald Breckenridge, author of *This Young Girl Passing*

"Carl Watson's work is desolate poetry. He writes with sharp nostalgia for a past that really wasn't all that great. It feels like a stay in a down-and-out motel, but right on the other side of the paper-thin wall is transcendence. Watson never lets you forget that even in the most desperate situations, there is humor (even if it's mostly black) and greatness of the spirit."

—Emily XYZ, contributor, *United States of Poetry*

Black & White on Paper | 6" x 9" | 238 pgs. | ISBN/EAN13: 0983927146 / 978-0983927143 | List: $15.95

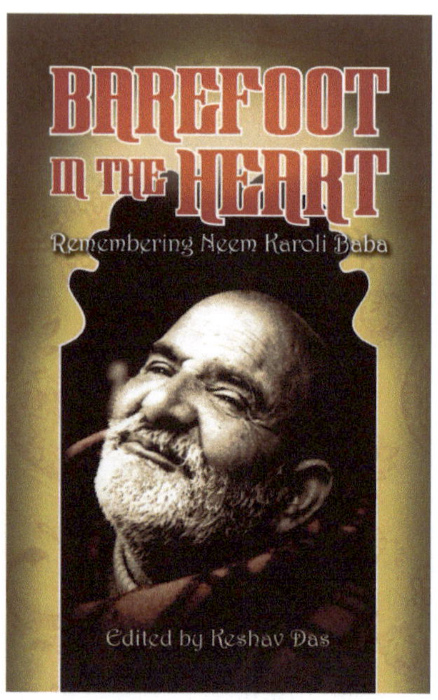

Barefoot in the Heart is a collection of transcribed oral stories of the Indian saint Neem Karoli Baba (Maharaji). It includes many anecdotes and first-person retellings of stories collected in India and in the USA over a period of 9 years by Keshav Das, including a small selection of unpublished stories originally intended for inclusion in *Miracle Of Love* by Ram Dass.

"*Barefoot in the Heart* is a divine raft to take us across the ocean of darkness to the glorious land of light. Every page is filled with Maharaji's nectar. Profound gratitude to Keshav Das and his collaborators."

—Jai Uttal

Black & White on Paper | 6" x 9" | 168 pgs. | ISBN-13/ISBN-10: 978-0983927129 / 098392712X | List: $15.95

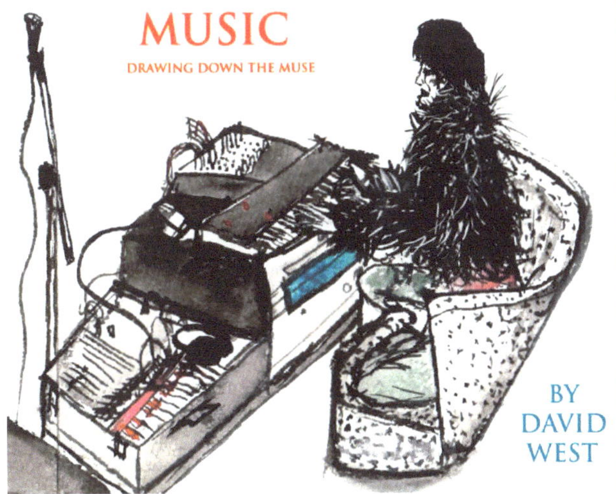

"Inside this book you get *portraiture vérité* of bands in action. Banging away in rehearsal. The appreciative eye watching the battle of the bands as they try to navigate their way through the sometimes complicated maze of illusions, delusions and solutions of grandeur before asphyxiation and evaporation of all the notes into the air.

"David West hits the target dead center BOOM with his beautifully liquid renderings of NYC bands in rehearsal. Mr. West captures a scene in the late 1990s largely ignored. These aren't vacuous American Idols but musicians who are The Real Deal. Like a fly on the wall, David gives you an inside view from his own multifaceted eye. There is a dripping aquatic fluidity to his drawings. Mr. West is not afraid to let the ink, gouache, and watercolor run and flow, never betraying the nature of his medium. That's why he's The Real Deal. If you the viewer can't understand, appreciate and see that in his work then go out and get corrective eye surgery!"

—Monte Cazazza of Psychic TV

Full Color Bleed on White paper | 8" x 7" | 110 pgs. | ISBN/EAN13: 0983927170 / 978-0983927174 | List: $24.95

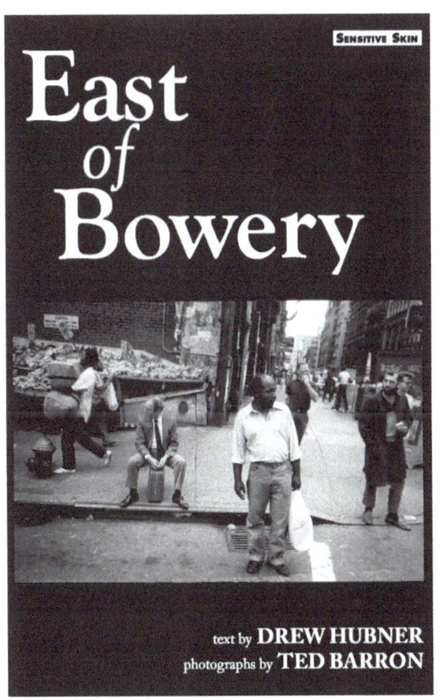

East of Bowery began as a collaborative web project between writer Drew Hubner (*American by Blood, We Pierce*) and photographer Ted Barron in 2008. It was subsequently performed as a multimedia event with live musical accompaniment at The Gershwin Hotel and The Bowery Poetry Club. This is the first print publication of the project.

"Drew Hubner's prose and Ted Barron's photos are kin, at once raw and lyrical, grit and grace, which is what the city was like back then. The combination is magic, the essence of the time and place."

—Luc Sante, author of *Low Life* and *Kill All Your Darlings*

"*East of Bowery* is a sharply focused, street-level view of Downtown before the real estate agents started renaming everything."

—Steve Earle, author of *Doghouse Roses* and *I'll Never Get out of This World Alive*

"Drew Hubner writes like people used to."

—William Georgiades, *New York Magazine*

"The voice is loose, jazzy and fast, the memories liquid and hot, avoiding the romance of macho drug memoirs with black humor, verisimilitude and a knack for the absurd."

—Kate Christensen, author of *In the Drink* and *The Astral*

Black & White on Paper | 6" x 9" | 154 pgs. | ISBN/EAN13: 0983927103 / 9780983927105| List: $15.95

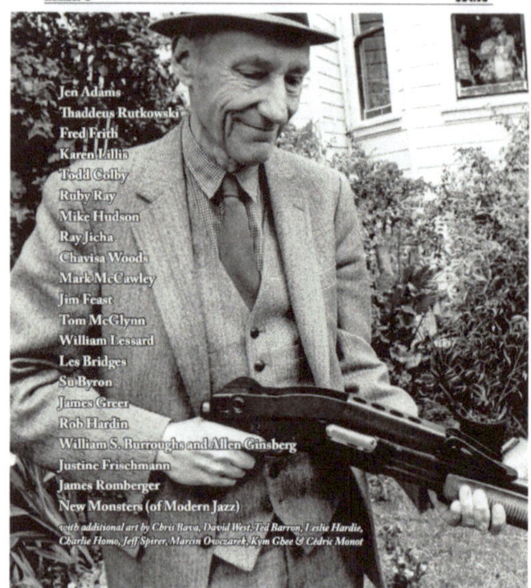

SENSITIVE SKIN #8

on sale at Amazon.com and select bookstores
PDF version available at sensitiveskinmagazine.com/downloads/sensitive-skin-8/

Featuring a rarely seen interview with **William S. Burroughs** by **Allen Ginsberg.**

With iconic punk photographs by **Ruby Ray**, art by **Tom McGlynn** and **Justine Frischmann**, music by **The New Monsters**, a comic written and drawn by **James Romberger**, writing by **Mike Hudson, James Greer, Thaddeus Rutkowski, Chavisa Woods, Jim Feast, Mark McCawley, Todd Colby** and much more.

Full Color on White Paper | 8.5" x 11" | 118 pgs. | ISBN-13: 978-0983927150 | ISBN-10: 0983927154 | List: $24.95

SENSITIVE SKIN #9

on sale at Amazon.com and select bookstores
PDF version available at sensitiveskinmagazine.com/downloads/sensitive-skin-9/

SENSITIVE SKIN
The World's Greatest Journal of Art, Literature and Music!
Number 9 $19.95

John Lurie/Samuel Delany/Vladimir Mayakovsky/James Romberger
Fred Frith/Marty Thau/Larissa Shmailo/Darius James/Doug Rice/
and much, much more…

Featuring an exclusive interview with, and music by, seminal guitarist **Fred Frith** (Henry Cow), the missing chapter from the latest novel by science fiction legend **Samuel R. Delaney,** and a portfolio of paintings from actor *(Stranger Than Paradise)* and musician (Lounge Lizards) **John Lurie.**

Plus a memoir by **Marty Thau,** former manager of Suicide and The New York Dolls, new translation of poetry by **Vladimir Mayakovsky** from **Jenny Wade,** photographs of the seamy side of Tijuana by **Chris Bava** and an interview with **Darius James,** conducted by **Ghazi Barakat,** about his documentary, *The United States of Hoodoo.*

The front cover is by reknowned illustrator **JD King,** and the back cover features a comic written and drawn by **James Romberger.** There's more writing by **Doug Rice, Susan Scutti, Larissa Shmailo, Bradley Spinelli, Anna Mockler, Jesus Angel Garcia** and **Aman Sabet,** as well as art by **Ha Young Kim, Marcin Owczarek, John Griffin, David West** and **Justine Frischmann,** and photographs by **Ted Barron, Ruby Ray, Hal Hirshorn, N.D. Koster** and **Geoffrey Ithen.**

Full Color on White Paper | 8.5" x 11" | 102 pgs. | ISBN-13: 978-0983927167 | ISBN-10: 0983927162 | List: $24.95

Sensitive Skin #10

on sale at Amazon.com and select bookstores
PDF version available at sensitiveskinmagazine.com/downloads/sensitive-skin-10/

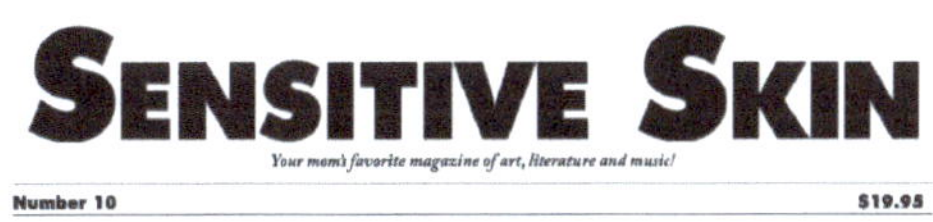

The issue features outtakes from the Wall Street collection by famed photographer **Charles Gatewood** (*Sidetripping, Forbidden Photographs*), fiction by downtown legends **Gary Indiana** (*Scar Tissue and Other Stories, White Trash, Horse Crazy, Gone Tomorrow*), **Max Blagg** (*Ticket Out*) and **Drew Hubner** (*East of Bowery*), plus work by Dead Kennedy roadie and junky bankrobber **Patrick O'Neil** (*The Hold-Up*), radio host **Tony DuShane** (*Confessions of a Teenage Jesus Jerk*), newcomer **E.A. Fow** and South American novelist **Raul Serrano Sanchez** (*Catálogo de ilusiones*), with poetry by Flarf pioneer **Sharon Mesmer** (*Annoying Diabetic Bitch, The Virgin Formica*), **Ron Kolm** (*Divine Comedy*), **Pete Simonelli** (*Night Sees You First, A Lonely War*) and **Michael Randall**, essays by **James Reich** (*Bombshell* and *I, Judas*), **Ronald B. Richardson** (*Narrative Madness*), cinema of transgression co-founder **Nick Zedd** and South African activist **Breyten Breytenback** (*The True Confessions of an Albino Terrorist*). Includes paintings by **Peter Shear**, music by **Steve Adams** (ROVA Saxophone Quartet) and more.

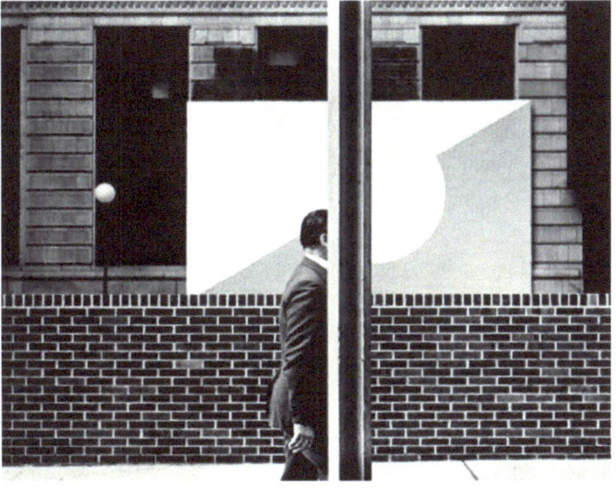

Charles Gatewood/Gary Indiana/Sharon Mesmer/Nick Zedd/
Peter Shear/Patrick O'Neil/Max Blagg/Tony DuShane
and much, much more . . .

Full Color on White Paper | 8.5" x 11" | 120 pgs. | ISBN-13: 978-0983927181 | ISBN-10: 0983927189 List: $24.95

SENSITIVE SKIN
Art, music and writing by and for people with ADHD, OCD, PTSD, LSD, OMG and WTF
Number 11 $24.95

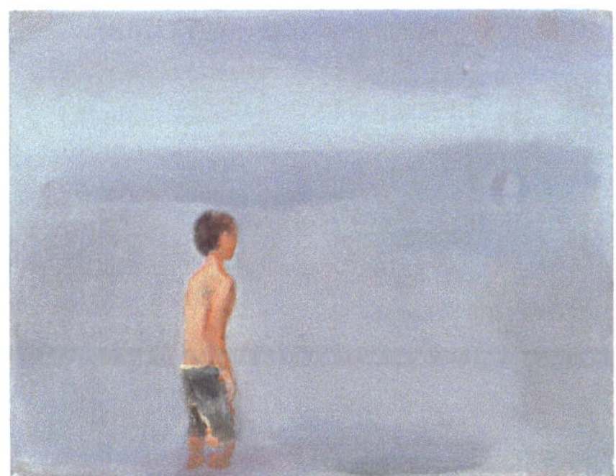

Maggie Estep/Alan Kaufman/Deborah Pintonelli/Stephen Lack
Evelyn Bencicova/Joshua Mohr/Celia Farber/Steve Dalachinsky
Arthur Nersesian/Marian St. Laurent/Margarita Shalina/Marc Olmsted

Sensitive Skin #11

on sale at Amazon.com and select bookstores
PDF version available at:
sensitiveskinmagazine.com/downloads/sensitive-skin-11/

Features writing by **Arthur Nersesian** (*The Fuck-Up*), Spin columnist **Celia Farber, Maggie Estep** (*Diary of an Emotional Idiot, Hex, Alice Fantastic*), **D. Scot Miller** (*Knot Frum Hear*), **Deborah Pintonelli** (*Ego Monkey*), **Joshua Mohr** (*Damascus, Fight Song*), **Anonymous** (*Diary of an Oxygen Thief*), **Alan Kaufman** (*Drunken Angel, Matches*) and **Marc Olmsted**, with an interview with **Dîre McCain**, editor of *Paraphilia Magazine*, by **Edward Robinson**.

We also have a great portfolio of paintings from East Village icon **Stephen Lack**, as well as photographs by **Gretchen Faust, Dennis Gordon** and **Evelyn Bencicova**, and live music from **Sun Ra**, recorded in NYC's Central Park in 1986.

Plus poetry by legend **Steve Dalachinsky** (*Fool's Gold*), **Sparrow, Lynn McGee, Rebecca Weiner Tompkins** (*Night Sees You First, A Lonely War*) and **Vladislav Khodosevic** (translated by **Jenny Wade**), an essay on post-collapse America, as seen in *True Detective*, by **Marian St. Laurent**.

Full Color on White Paper | 8.5" x 11" | 130 pgs. | ISBN-13: 978-0983927198 | ISBN-10: 0983927197 List: $24.95

SENSITIVE SKIN #12

on sale at Amazon.com and select bookstores
PDF version available at sensitiveskinmagazine.com/downloads/sensitive-skin-12/

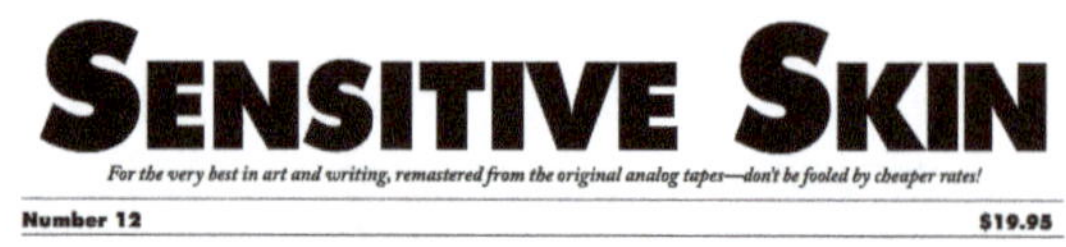

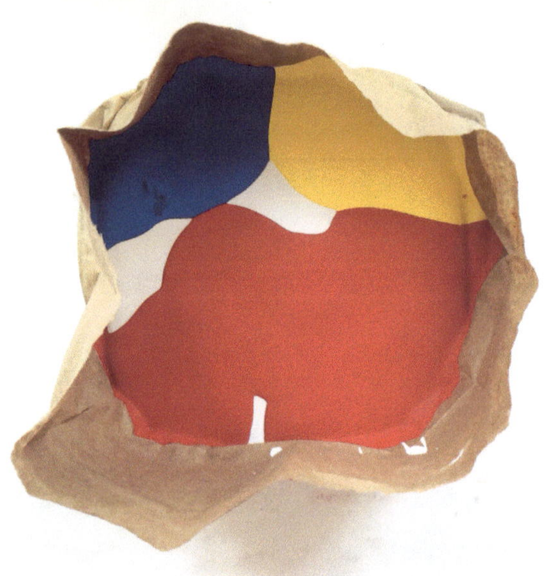

Jack Micheline/Bob Holman/Wanda Phipps/John Lurie/Emily XYZ/Charles Gatewood/ Winston Smith/Justine Frischmann/Hal Sirowitz/Taylor Mead/Sharon Mesmer/ Vladimir Mayakovsky/John S. Hall/Rebecca Weiner Tompkins/David Rattray/ Ruby Ray/Jean-Christian Bourcart/Stephen Lack/Carl Watson/JD King and many, many more . . .

Published April 2015, a special issue in celebration of Poetry Month. 30 poems (one for every day in April) by **John S. Hall, Bonny Finberg, JD King, Emily XYZ, Marc Olmsted, Jack Micheline, Jose Padua, Michael Randall, Ron Kolm, Pete Simonelli, Bob Holman, Hal Sirowitz, Sparrow, steve dalachinsky, Wanda Phipps, Eddie Woods, Max Blagg, Larissa Shmaillo, Rob Hardin, Rebecca Weiner Tompkins, Ron Richardson, Carl Watson, John Farris, David Rattray, Norman Douglas, Sharon Mesmer, Taylor Mead, Michael Carter, Vladimir Mayakovsky** and **Sean Flaherty.**

Accompanying the poems is art by **Rick Prol, Charles Gatewood, JD King, Henner Schroeder, Jonathan Cowan, John Lurie, Liz Kresch, Kym Ghee, Daniel Kolm, Jean-Christian Bourcart, David de Biasio, Clinton King, Samoa, Tom McGlynn, Chris Bava, Evelyn Bencicova, Peter Shear, David West, Leslie Hardie, Joseph O'Neal, Ted Barron, Charles Schick, Dennis Gordon, Hal Hirshorn, Ruby Ray, Marina Loeb, Stephen Lack, Justin Rhody, Justine Frischmann** and **Jeff Spirer.**

The front cover is by Brooklyn painter and curator Julie Torres, and the back cover is by the legendary graphic artist Winston Smith.

Full Color on White Paper | 8.5" x 11" | 82 pgs. | ISBN-13: 978-0996157001 | ISBN-10: 099615700X List: $19.95

www.ingramcontent.com/pod-product-compliance
Lightning Source LLC
LaVergne TN
LVHW070132110826
845147LV00002B/236